BEN PINNINGTON

MAKING WAVES

PR strategies to transform
your maritime business

Rethink

First published in Great Britain in 2021
by Rethink Press (www.rethinkpress.com)

© Copyright Ben Pinnington

Dedicated to my grandparents Mary and Philip Lloyd,
who loved the sea

Contents

Foreword

Does maritime need modernising? In the pre-Covid-19 days, you could visit a trade show and see plenty of evidence of new technology displayed in high-tech booths, with all the marketing collateral you would ever want. The stands were selling products and services to an industry that delivers world trade to our doorsteps in twenty- to thirty-year-old ships. The traditional 'sea blindness' that affects the industry has perhaps been lifted a little by the pandemic and rare events like the Suez Canal blockage. The aging ships delivering our goods are a country mile from being 'digitalised' and 'decarbonised'. It is these very ships and this very industry that must be turned around by order of United Nations legislation, fed down via the International Maritime Organization. This is a huge task, with many sceptics in tow doubting whether targets can be met.

This Herculean task, though, provides businesses with an opportunity to adapt, innovate and grow. The initial developers of solutions will be government backed or multinationals with pockets deep enough to invest for the medium to long term. As the curve of adoption rises, the market grows, and more opportunities will reveal themselves to those who are prepared.

Gaining market share with a margin high enough to sustain and grow the business will come down to convincing clients and prospects that your product or service is cheaper, faster or better. To make headway and win market share, one of these three must be the case, but there is also the hugely important task of communicating to the market the fact you are there. All that innovation will be for nought if the communications is left out of the plan. Public relations starts with a grounded understanding of your company and your offer. It helps set your agenda and your key messages.

Ben Pinnington's book, Making Waves, will broaden the vision of PR and marketing professionals who want to deepen their knowledge of the industry. The even bigger audience, however, will be the large army of SMEs out there who are innovating, researching and bringing new products and services to market. The C-suite managers of these enterprises need independent guidance on the valuable tool that is public relations. So often, they come from a sales, operations or finance background, without the broad overview and insight required. This book will steer them in the right direction and provide them with the insight to successfully implement a communications strategy.

Ask yourself: how do you want to be viewed in five years' time? Or ten? How will you communicate your own 'cheaper, better, faster'? This book will show you how.

Tom Chant
CEO, Society of Maritime Industries

Introduction

J ust after finishing university in the late 1990s, I had an office job in Liverpool, near my parents' home. It was a monochrome time and money was tight as I saved up to go to journalism college in Cornwall. The one redeeming factor was the office's position overlooking the River Mersey. During our breaks the team would gather in a room with a huge window, with beautiful panoramic views of the fast-moving river. There was something so inspiring about looking out at the ships and historic port buildings, especially at dusk. One of the older bosses liked to chat about his time as a seafarer and the two of us would often talk about sailing from Liverpool to New York. Exploring the world seemed a distant prospect to me then when I had to focus on starting my career. Little did I know that the answer to my dreams of days of purpose, adventure and cities glittering faraway lay in the furious waves below.

Why PR?

For a long time, I was not sure how to write a book about public relations (PR) that would be different. My lightbulb moment came when I was riding my bike near my home in Didsbury: PR in the maritime sector. To my knowledge, no one has covered this particular angle before, and I could draw on a unique set of experiences.

I have written this book as a companion to the industry I have fallen in love with. What it is not is an academic-style PR book. *Making Waves* is more a hybrid book, blending theory with the practical realities of running a PR firm in a sector where the market is brutally honest.

The experiences I share in *Making Waves* are drawn mainly from the business sector, where commitment to and understanding of PR is different to that in politics or the public sector. To a degree, there is a valley of death between textbook PR theory and what some maritime companies are prepared to embrace. While my company, Polaris, has worked for companies and organisations that 'get' PR, we have also worked with businesses, both private and state owned, that do not fully harness or understand PR, seeing it as a luxury, a risk or on-off tactical tool. PR campaigns expire in this arid valley and companies put themselves at a considerable disadvantage by failing to maximise PR.

Making Waves is in part a response to this. Using theory alongside real-world case studies, it will explain why PR matters as a strategic tool fundamental to maritime business operations.

The maritime industry is going through immense change and needs to communicate better in these progressive times. PR professionals and maritime businesses and organisations have a significant challenge to come together like a rising tide to lift the general standard of communication in the sector.

Making Waves is not a complete guide to marketing and communications, either. That is too vast a canvas, so I have decided to focus primarily on external communications but with a clear acknowledgement of the need to set objectives for PR campaigns for maritime businesses and organisations of all sizes. The research I have undertaken draws me to the conclusion that the organisations which are clear on why they are engaging in PR and how they are going to manage and measure it will be the most successful.

Too often, campaigns fall down in this planning phase. *Making Waves* is designed to arm you with the knowledge and tools to execute success.

Why maritime?

Maritime is not Polaris' only sector, but it is our biggest, and it has given me and the Polaris team so much. From our modest beginnings as a startup PR firm in our home port of Liverpool, with a maxed-out credit card and a bank overdraft, we have been lucky enough to grow and travel the world, exceeding the expectations of some naysayer advisers. The best thing I have ever done in business is set up a company and diversify overseas, catching a trade wind to exciting new lands.

Today, exports account for a third of Polaris' income, and we have grown from a local company to having a national and international client base. My dream was to see the world, learn from different cultures and countries, gain contacts and create opportunities for Polaris and our clients. And that is the gift that maritime, as an export-driven sector, keeps offering.

We have collected unforgettable memories, from promoting sun-baked ceremonies at Oman Drydock in the remote desert wilderness of Duqm, to pitching to the Maharana of Mewar over gin and tonic on the roof of an ancient palace in Udaipur, to trips around the glorious old town and ramshackle shipyards of Gdansk, to flying into Shanghai to promote the British Pavilion at Marintec, marking 150 years of Lloyd's Register in China.

Closer to home, I draw experience from a 13-year retained relationship with iconic shipbuilder Cammell Laird, before the company's management changes marked the end of an era. This period saw my team and I being bounced from the *Today* programme to announce the return of the famous name in 2008 to major press events with Sir David Attenborough and the Duke and Duchess of Cambridge. It was one hell of a ride on the Thunder Road of shipbuilding, but more than anything, I loved the passion of the place: stereos blasting out The Clash in huge shipbuilding halls that were buzzing with energy, wit and humour, the workforce like one big rowdy family. It all made incredible material for the media and was utterly intoxicating, and it taught me many lessons.

The challenges facing maritime

For all the love so many people have for maritime, it is not an industry without challenges. Yes, it is fundamental to global trade, but traditionally male-dominated and conservative, it can be old school and has a habit of trying to keep out of the news and away from scrutiny. Maritime has a big job to do to communicate outside its bubble, and in some ways, it is only willing to change under pressure, as we have seen with the decarbonisation agenda. This long-overdue agenda is demanding that maritime companies show publicly that they are taking action to slash emissions after years of procrastination.

The green fuel issue is symptomatic of the challenges the industry faces. For years, it chucked some of the worst quality 'bunker' fuel – essentially, the dregs of the refining process, producing noxious gases and harmful fine particles – into ships because it was cheap. Seafarers, meanwhile, are now mostly drawn from the developing world, notably India and the Philippines, because they offer cheap labour and are often willing to take on one of the most dangerous, lonely jobs on earth to support their families. How seafarers have been taken for granted was shown in the crew change crisis during the Covid pandemic.[1] Governments have tended to look the other way, forcing seafarers to endure extended contracts and unacceptably long periods away from their loved ones. The spectre of seafarer depression, self-harm and, tragically, suicide hangs over shipping like a long, dark shadow.

Maritime has a long way to go to address the troubling sides to the industry, but change is happening, and it is heartening to see media like *Seatrade Maritime* and *Lloyd's List* and powerful bodies like the International Maritime Organization (IMO) take a lead to shine a spotlight on seafarer welfare. In addition, there is a concerted effort to encourage greater gender diversity in the sector. This is desperately needed to break maritime away from its comfortable boys' club and use the different skillsets and perspectives women can bring.

When I first worked in maritime, I was struck by the hierarchical, loyal, generous, blunt and sometimes abrasive nature of some of the businesses I worked in. Operations came first, and marketing and communications were some way behind. The senior leaders had limited knowledge of PR and how to manage it, and many had not used professional PR before.

This was in stark contrast to the time I had spent working in politics and lobbying, where the media and the organisation's profile were fundamental. In the commercial world, it seemed that corporate businesses and professional services firms were most savvy about PR and marketing, devoting significant budget and senior management time to it. Maritime appeared caught in a slight time warp where it viewed the media with suspicion or disinterest. The idea of having PR plans and teams focused on brand and reputation was not a priority.

That outlook has changed in recent years, helped by the power of social media, which is shaking up boardrooms. Company leaders who saw social media as a dubious fad back in 2008 now recognise its astonishing power, especially among their staff and stakeholders. But there is still a long way to go for PR to be fully recognised in the maritime sector. The older leaders may be shrewd, but like an oil tanker, they turn slowly and too often prefer a low profile and to stay in the shadows. This is an aberration in modern times, when businesses are expected to stand up and be counted in the face of enormous scrutiny and to show what they believe in.

My fear is that too many maritime businesses, particularly in the SME supply chain, are trapped in *reengineering* the past of diesel engine ships when they could be *reverse engineering* the future of clean fuel ships and digitisation. These businesses risk being left behind, unless they show they are embracing the future in their operations and PR.

The reality of running a business

The insights in *Making Waves* are drawn from years of being out there in the 'wide ocean', doing the job, sometimes battling towering seas, sometimes cruising into a sunset of dreams. The know-how I am sharing is born from running a boutique PR firm working for maritime businesses of all sizes around the world. I have also spoken with leading PR figures and undertaken the excellent training courses with the Chartered Institute of Public Relations (CIPR) to ensure what I am sharing is practical and up to date.

However, I do not want to over-sanitise our experiences. At Polaris we have worked hard, faced adversity, and experienced our own share of agony and ecstasy. Without these triumphs and setbacks, moments of inspiration and disappointment, I would not be qualified to write this book.

Running a business is a way of life. It can be rewarding, but it is hard. You need emotional resilience to sail through bad weather, otherwise you will feel every big wave hit your hull. It is a stark reality that every business will face failure and pain, and unless you can see each down moment as an up, an opportunity to learn, recalibrate and get better, business is not for you. It is often the people who are in business to show off, or who have never failed – those who enjoyed straight As in education – who find the brutal nature of entrepreneurship hardest.

Business will rough you up – not every client will be loyal, despite your best endeavours, and team members and business partners will not always work out. And you will make mistakes. But with setbacks comes the opportunity for renewal. You will find new team members and new clients whose values are more aligned to your own. It is in the moments when you face genuine hardship, when you step out of your comfort zone, that you really learn.

Adversity, when it has come along, has actually helped Polaris evolve and improve. In tougher periods, I have found out more about who I am and, critically, what the company is about and why ethos matters. Adversity has also underlined to me that a business is only as good as its team, and I have been lucky to find the right people to support Polaris. Our strapline is 'Passion for PR' and I write it on the worksheet each day. Passion informs our outlook and everything we do.

Passion in PR is fundamental. In a way, that is rule one: do not get into maritime unless you feel passionate about it, otherwise you will find the trade wind quickly dies from your sails, and you are likely to lose interest and motivation. You need to do your client's story justice. If your PR consultancy or in-house team cannot do this, it is time to change.

The maritime sector is too vibrant, too full of passionate people. You have to find advisers in your business who are electrified by maritime; only then can you be competitive enough to stand out. The adage of employing people who are better than you is absolutely true. I can see this when I look at the difference capable people have made to clients and at Polaris. The ability to deliver in PR, in my experience, comes not from the mega-talented superstars, but from those who are prepared to combine their training, skill and passion with really bending their backs. Give me a grafter over a superstar every time.

In recent times Polaris has evolved embracing more self-employed talent to bolster our team, and we see this more and more in the creative industry. With the increase in remote working and self-employment, we seek out teams of highly skilled expert freelancers to support us on a retained or project basis. This is more effective for client delivery than drawing from a smaller number of full-time people and being limited to their skills set. PR companies that adopt this agile new business model and embrace the flexible freelance talent pool are finding they have a competitive edge. As we well know, the self-employed bring an edge; we must deliver to survive. There is never any room for complacency in the small business world.

Who is this book for?

This book is written for the C-suite and PR and marketing teams of maritime businesses, large and small. These are the people my team is lucky enough to support every day. I want this book to be a guide, offering the answers and methods you need to maximise your PR potential and protect you in a crisis.

'Crisis' is a scary word. It may not happen to your business, or it may happen extremely rarely, but with preparation, you could foresee and prevent it, making sure the crisis never happens. This is one of the most effective forms of crisis PR. And if you are hit by a 'big one', preparation and a tested plan will give you a good idea of how to handle it.

The importance of the maritime media

PR in the maritime industry is changing extremely quickly, driven by social media and tech. But in PR and business, it is important to see, know and build a rapport with clients, journalists and contacts, and you cannot rely on social media alone to do that. It is a facilitator and communication tool, but trust is built in person, seeing the whites of your contact's eyes, reading their body language and finding shared common interests. That is one reason why the brilliant international maritime trade fairs play such a key role; maritime is a global but tight-knit community. Many of the best opportunities in the future will come to those who have an international profile network of real contacts.

The international maritime press is one of the largest and most vibrant and diverse of any sector in the world. There are many dedicated journalists who, like the maritime PRs, are utterly in love with maritime. Its media is a paradise for promotion with daily newsletters, websites, social media feeds and print magazines, but many maritime companies fail to harness this reach as a porthole window to the world. Those who do reap huge rewards.

Maritime is a sector that is built on travel, export and interconnected supply chains. Polaris has seen real growth in international work, supporting clients like Oman Shipping, the Port of Gdansk and China Classification Society. We now work with businesses in a way which would have been impossible without tech. It enables ease of communication with free emails and WhatsApp calls, and helps us to solve major PR problems for international maritime businesses and find new markets beyond a business's existing contact networks by raising global awareness in English, which remains the primary language of the maritime industry. Most of the maritime press is written in English, so if you are a maritime business eager to export you cannot afford to stand still. It is vital to embrace the reach of the vibrant maritime press as part of a fully developed communications plan.

1
The Maritime Industry

The maritime industry is a curious beast. It is the backbone of the global economy with more than 50,000 merchant ships traversing the oceans, manned by around 1.6 million seafarers transporting around 12 billion tonnes of seaborne trade, accounting for nearly 90 per cent of all visible world trade in 2021 according to Clarksons Research.[2] Crucially, the industry is on an upward trajectory and on course to double in value from $1,500 billion in 2010 to $3,000 billion by 2030.[3]

Yet despite its riveting heritage, so intertwined with exploration and the development of humankind, its exciting future and its buccaneering nature, maritime is often out of sight and out of mind to the general public. 'Sea blindness' is spoken about as a big problem in the industry, not helped by many maritime organisations' antiquated approach to PR and preference to remain anonymous and low profile. There is a common ignorance about the role of shipping and the fact it transports the stuff we need to live: medicine, food, oil, coal, gas, timber, iron ore, grain, vehicles, electronics, machinery, clothes and so on.

Supremacy of the seas, which cover 70 per cent of the world's surface, remains the determining factor in the global balance of power, as it has done for centuries. All major countries need access to the sea to survive and receive the goods they cannot mine, make or grow for themselves, as well as sustain and expand their economies by selling the things they can to overseas markets. If Britain, for example, had lost the Battle of the Atlantic in World War Two, it would almost certainly have capitulated to Nazi Germany, unable to arm, fuel or feed itself. There would have been no supplies for the Eastern Front in Russia or North Africa and no D-Day. Dominance of the seas was arguably the critical factor in the outcome of the war.[4]

To underline the importance of the sea, China is investing huge resources into its maritime industry as it seeks never to be dominated and exploited again by superior maritime powers as it was in the 19th century. As a result, in the last 20 years, China has grown into a maritime superpower and its naval fleet is now the largest in the world. Reuters reports that China has 400 warships and submarines compared to the United

States' (albeit technically superior) 288, with projections the Chinese fleet could grow to 530 by 2030.[5]

This has major implications not just for the South China Seas, but longer term for the Indian Ocean and the Pacific. Better communications can play a role in strengthening and ameliorating relationships between China and the West. Leading historian Kerry Brown discusses the need to learn more about China and Chinese history. In his book *China*, Brown says: 'However marginal China may have seemed in much of the period since the mid-19th century, for a country and a culture accounting for a fifth of humanity, its story is a global one. It was an aberration that so little of the story was known outside of China. What we are witnessing now is a long overdue correction to this imbalance.'[6]

China is effectively restoring its place as an economic superpower, and nowhere is this seen more clearly than in the maritime industry. Positive engagement and dialogue are essential in maritime as China is now central to so many aspects of this industry, and as the world's second biggest economy, it is not going anywhere.

Maritime matters

More widely, it is incumbent on the entire industry to help drive positive public awareness of the importance of maritime. This is a big focus of the Maritime Foundation, which works hard to highlight the efforts of writers, journalists and film makers in the maritime field each year at its annual awards in London. The benefits are manifold, from encouraging more young people to consider exciting careers in the sector to lobbying politicians to ramp up support for maritime as a fundamental wealth creator. But despite the efforts of the Society of Maritime Industries, it is a long-running bugbear of mine to see underinvestment in UK pavilions at the magnificent maritime trade fairs around the world, while the likes of Germany, the Netherlands, Denmark and Norway blaze a trail with often heavily subsidised pavilions packed with exhibitors.

One of the prime reasons that maritime matters, particularly in Britain, is the opportunity it offers in a post-Brexit, post-Covid world. The sector is at the heart of globalisation, evidenced by the gigantic impact of population growth on seaborne trade. Between 1950 and 2011, the world's population grew from 2.2 billion to 6.9 billion.[7] As a result, seaborne trade quadrupled in the last four decades of that period, and now accounts for 12 billion tons of goods worth more than $14 trillion[8] being transported by ship each year.

And this growth in maritime is set to continue, driven by massive changes in ship and port technology combined with the predicted expansion of the global population. A vast two-year study, The Global Marine Trends 2030 Report published in 2013 by Lloyd's

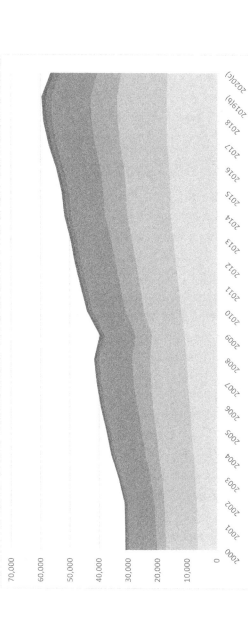

International maritime trade in cargo ton-miles, 2000–2020 (estimated billions of ton-miles)[9]

Legend: ■ Main bulk (a) ■ Other dry cargo ■ Container ■ Oil ■ Gas ■ Chemicals

a: Includes iron ore, grain, coal, bauxite/alumina and phosphate. Starting in 2006, 'main bulk' includes iron ore, grain and coal only. Data relating to bauxite/alumina and phosphate are included under 'other dry cargo'.

b: Estimated

c: Forecast

Register and the University of Strathclyde, found that seaborne trade could rise to somewhere between 19 and 24 billion tonnes by 2030 as the global population grows from 6.9 billion in 2010 to an estimated 8 billion by 2030 – 96 per cent of growth coming from developing countries.[10] In a world before Covid, the study found that this would drive massive growth with global gross domestic product (GDP) increasing by up to three times between 2010 and 2030, and I do not anticipate these findings changing significantly post-Covid. This in turn would create enormous opportunities for the marine industry due to the supply and demand for resources, technologies, goods and services. As a result, there will be huge volumes of work for shipyards and equipment manufacturers to build and maintain additional new tonnage for a wide range of ships, from container vessels for transporting manufactured goods to bulkers and tankers for commodity trades.

In addition, the report states that more people means a greater need for energy, with an estimated 40 per cent increase in energy demand by 2030 compared to 2010. This means more drill ships for ever deeper oil and gas fields. Offshore wind capacity, according to a report from the Global Wind Energy Council, is set to skyrocket from 29.1 gigawatts (gw) at the end of 2019 to more than 234 gw by 2030, led by growth in the Asia-Pacific region and continued growth in Europe.[11]

In 2020, there were record offshore wind capacity startups and project sanctioning, according to Clarksons Research. The UK was the largest producer in 2020 but is now being overtaken by China.[12] According to Bloomberg New Energy Finance, China built more than half of the world's new wind power capacity in 2020. Its onshore and offshore windfarms grew by almost 58 gw, more than the world's combined wind power growth in 2019.[13] In total, the report found developers built almost 100 gw worth of windfarms globally in 2020 – a rise of nearly 60 per cent on 2019.

It is because of this type of growth that the Organisation for Economic Co-operation and Development (OECD) predicted, pre-Covid, that the maritime sector could double in size between 2010 and 2030 to be worth $3,000 billion.[14] Again, I do not believe that these findings will change significantly post-Covid, so they remain relevant in today's altered world. The UK as an island nation is well placed to harvest this growth.

The UK maritime sector is in good health. It drove £46.1 billion in gross value added in 2017, a £8.3 billion increase since 2010, making maritime larger than rail and aerospace. Maritime further directly supports 220,100 jobs in Britain, an increase of 24,000 jobs from 2010.[15]

The importance of Asia

As the forces of globalisation continue to reverberate, it will be important to engage with Asia as the world's economic centre moves eastwards. Asia's middle class is forecast to add two billion additional consumers by 2030.[16] The Global Marine Trends 2030 study predicts that India will overtake China as having the largest population and the largest labour force in the world, and by 2030, the largest economies, by a long way, will be China, the USA and India.

The report found that the countries with the largest growth in per-capita GDP (an important measure of purchasing power and labour cost) will be China, Vietnam, India and Indonesia. Purchasing power in developing Asia will rise eight times between 2010 and 2030.

The irresistible rise of China as the apex maritime superpower is also set to continue. Having opened up its economy in 1978, China now leads the world in seaborne trade, shipbuilding and integrated ownership and ship management. The 2018 Leading Maritime Nations of the World report produced by DNV and Menon Economics says China is number one thanks to it being immensely strong in ship owning, ship finance, ship management and shipbuilding.[17] It controls more than 40 per cent of global shipbuilding, predicted to increase to as much as 55 per cent by 2030 by the Global Marine Trends report.

When Polaris promoted the British Pavilion with the Society of Maritime Industries at the Marintec trade fair in Shanghai in 2019, we reported that China is home to more than 400 ship owners and 133 shipyards with, at that time, a staggering 1,483 ships on their order books. In addition, China dominates port operations, being home to seven of the ten largest ports in the world.

This breathtaking transformation of China's maritime industry is expected to see even greater growth in its commercial fleet ownership, rivalling Greece and the rest of the European countries combined, although Greek ship owning remains strong. As of January 2018, the top ship-owning economies combined accounted for 52 per cent of world fleet tonnage. Greece held a market share of 18 per cent, followed by China and Hong Kong (16 per cent), Japan (11 per cent), and Singapore (seven per cent). Half of the world's tonnage was owned by Asian companies. Owners from Europe accounted for 41 per cent and from Northern America for six per cent.[18]

Japan's high rank in shipping can be attributed to its strong concentration of ship owners and managers, with three of the largest shipping companies in the world, K Line, Nippon Yusen Kaisha and MOL, based in the country. In terms of number of vessels, China commands the leading position, being home to 6,738 ships of 1,000 gross tons and above, followed by Greece with 4,199.[19]

Decarbonisation

A massive driver of the maritime industry, now and in the future, is the decarbonisation agenda. Although ocean transportation is seen as the least polluting mode of transport – reportedly, it is three times more environmentally friendly than land transport and fifteen times more than aviation – if the global shipping industry were a country, it would be the world's sixth-largest generator of carbon dioxide emissions, ahead of Germany, primarily due to the low quality of cheap 'bunker fuel'. According to Clarksons Research, the international shipping fleet produces over 800 million tonnes and around 2.4 per cent of global CO2 emissions.[20] Meanwhile, the cost of decarbonising the whole sector has been pitched at between $1.4 trillion and $1.9 trillion.

The IMO, an agency of the United Nations based in London that regulates shipping, is driving much-needed change to reduce air pollution from ships and improve energy efficiency. In 2011, the IMO adopted the first mandatory requirements for improving the energy efficiency of new-build ships worldwide. Meanwhile, from 1 January 2020, the IMO required that all fuels used in ships contain no more than 0.5 per cent sulphur.[21] The cap is a significant reduction from the previous sulphur limit of 3.5 per cent. Public health experts estimate that once the 2020 sulphur cap takes effect, it will prevent roughly 150,000 premature deaths and 7.6 million childhood asthma cases globally each year.[22]

In addition, in April 2018, the IMO adopted an initial strategy to reduce greenhouse gas (GHG) emissions from shipping by at least 50 per cent by 2050 compared to 2008 levels and 'phase them out, as soon as possible in this century'.[23] Another heavyweight initiative is the Getting to Zero Coalition, a powerful group of more than 150 of the leading names in maritime, including shipping lines, ports, original equipment manufacturers and classification societies. The coalition reports that to make the transition to full decarbonisation possible, commercially viable zero-emission vessels must start entering the global fleet by 2030, with their numbers radically scaled up through the 2030s and 2040s.[24] This can only be achieved through close collaboration between the maritime industry, the energy sector, the financial sector, governments and intergovernmental organisations.

Another initiative gaining traction is the Poseidon Principles. Launched in 2019 and consisting of eighteen lending institutions with a shipping portfolio of around $150 billion, it commits members to aligning their policies with climate considerations. The lenders assess the alignment of the emissions of their existing shipping portfolios with decarbonisation trajectories set out for each vessel in terms of size and type by the IMO GHG 2050 target.

To achieve this, lenders rely on ship owners to provide emissions data. The recent mood music from senior sources is that the signatories to the principles are serious, and failure to properly adapt diesel ships could soon see ship owners becoming 'stranded', unable to raise the mortgage to operate.

A key theme of this book is to encourage maritime businesses to embrace the decarbonisation agenda and digitisation revolution with greater conviction in their PR. These are the twin issues sweeping trade winds of change through the maritime industry, but while the maritime media brims with vitality on these subjects, it is not always reflected in businesses' communications. Too many companies and organisations remain silent on these issues, perhaps comfortable with fuel oil ships and the abundance of work that still exists in this fleet.

But this is emphatically *not* the future. It is imperative that companies set the right tone in their communications, reflecting the mood of the industry and the urgent need to act to tackle climate change.

Show how your business or organisation is innovating and adapting. If you stay stuck in a diesel rut, not only will your PR sound out of touch, but you are missing huge business opportunities. Look at the enormous value of decarbonisation and the efficiencies digitisation delivers. If you build more of your communications around these themes, opportunities will flow into your business like a fast-moving tide.

Key points

- Access to the seas will always be essential for countries so that they can both receive the goods they need to survive and trade with other lands.

- Forward-thinking countries such as China are investing heavily in their maritime presence.

- It will become increasingly important to engage with Asia as the world's economic centre moves eastwards.

- A massive driver of the maritime industry, both now and in the future, is the decarbonisation agenda.

- Maritime businesses need to embrace the decarbonisation agenda and digitisation revolution in their PR.

2
What Is PR?

During the research for this book, I have found myself increasingly thinking about and discussing what PR is in today's business world. What is the reality for CEOs, marketing teams and PR consultants? How does PR work in practice?

There can be considerable confusion about what is expected of PR. It is often seen as marketing or a sales tool, when in the purest sense, it is neither. As the late Sam Black, one of the pioneers of PR in Britain, set out in his celebrated work *The Essentials of Public Relations*,[25] PR is integral to the management of any organisation. It is not merely an add-on to marketing.

I would urge CEOs and executives to see PR as essential to the strategic direction of the organisation. For any PR campaign to work, it is vital that it has the support and understanding of the owner and C-suite of the business or organisation, otherwise it is unlikely to be a priority to anyone else. As an example of the importance of communications, look at how the Prime Minister's right-hand adviser is often a PR specialist – think Margaret Thatcher and Bernard Ingham or Tony Blair and Alistair Campbell.

What is PR?

Stripping it right back, what is PR? What are you investing in?

The Chartered Institute of Public Relations (CIPR) says:

'Every organisation, no matter how large or small, ultimately depends on its reputation for survival and success.

'Customers, suppliers, employees, investors, journalists and regulators can have a powerful impact. They all have an opinion about the organisations they come into contact with – whether good or bad, right or wrong. These perceptions will drive their decisions about whether they want to work with, shop with and support these organisations.

'In today's competitive market, reputation can be a company's biggest asset – the thing that makes it stand out from the crowd and gives it an edge. Effective PR can help manage reputation by communicating and building good relationships with all organisation stakeholders.'

The CIPR goes on to define PR:

'Public Relations is about reputation – the result of what you do, what you say and what others say about you.

'Public Relations is the discipline which looks after reputation, with the aim of earning understanding and support and influencing opinion and behaviour. It is the planned and sustained effort to establish and maintain goodwill and mutual understanding between an organisation and its publics.'[26]

Knowing how to make PR work

Businesses that succeed with PR thrust communications to their core and their CEOs embrace it – think Steve Jobs, Elon Musk and Richard Branson. They are all passionate about getting their message out and being the person leading it.

Businesses that maximise PR are clear on why they are engaging in it. They want profile, awareness and understanding; they want to influence and they want to build trust with clearly defined stakeholders. The trust point is critical because PR is *not* spin – ie distorting the truth by overstating your case. Good PR is rooted in truth – that is how you build reputation.

More widely, organisations that get PR right make the PR manager part of the senior leadership team and grasp the strategic value of communications. It is the job of a PR professional to proactively build relations with a company's stakeholders that really count.

They do this by explaining the CEO and company's vision, listening and providing feedback to senior management on the mood of stakeholders, the industry and society, so they can shape strategy accordingly. PR is as much about listening as it is about broadcasting a message. If organisations expect stakeholders to be influenced by what they say, they cannot simply transmit a message and expect people to believe in it. PR is a two-way conversation, and organisations have to show they are listening as well as talking, and that they are prepared to become an advocate of their stakeholders' messages. This is the essence of good PR and the key to building deeper relationships around shared values and outlook. As Anne Gregory points out in her book *Planning and Managing Public Relations Campaigns*,[27] 'Organisations that are not in touch with the public mood find themselves in difficulties whereas those that are in touch can have a significant advantage.' Gregory states PR is more than a tactical communications tool used purely to communicate information or add gloss – it is integral to the strategic development process.

For example, in the maritime industry, the United Nations Sustainable Development Goals are being used widely by leading organisations to shape their strategies. By reporting this kind of trend, a PR adviser can help guide a company as to the direction of the industry.

Another example could be a PR adviser providing counsel on a management decision to switch flag state – the jurisdiction under which a vessel is registered or licenced – to one that is cheaper. Here, the PR adviser can caution that this decision could affect the reputation of the ship owner as the intended flag state does not have a strong track record of supporting seafarer welfare, increasing the risk to seafarers and conflicting with the company's values. Furthermore, the PR team can keep a close eye on the behemoth that social media has become and feed back on 'hot' issues emerging that could affect the company – social media is an incredible listening tool as well as a promotional one.

In addition, businesses that succeed with PR know how they are going to manage and measure the campaign – from the outset. They understand publicity, and that media relations is a big part of it, but they also recognise that it covers the ethos of the business, what the company stands for and believes in, as well as its corporate and visual identity, and its own media channels, such as social media.

Challenging vague expectations

The reality in the business world is that companies will often grab at PR without really understanding it. PR firms bursting with energy and good intentions snap the deal up because they want the income, and then go out and make noise without agreeing clear objectives with the client. Sometimes this works; sometimes it does not. When it fails, it is usually because there is no communications plan with specific, measurable, achievable, relevant, time-bound (SMART) objectives and methods of evaluation.

In the commercial world, businesses can see PR as another way to drive sales and expect it to create leads without first and foremost understanding that it is about managing reputation, influencing attitudes and creating the right climate for a sales team. The PR consultant must take the time to explain what PR is to a business owner or CEO rather than run headlong into a campaign. If the client expects the PR consultant to generate leads, this requires clear, strategic thought, time and intelligent harvesting.

PR cannot work in a vacuum or silo. It must be measured against the campaign's starting point. What is the current profile of the business? How is it perceived, and how does it want to be known? What is the ethos of the company? How does it need to improve?

These are the pain points that, in my experience, cause most confusion and problems in PR campaigns. Get this strategy right and PR can deliver spectacular results, including building a good brand reputation by influencing the attitudes and behaviours of your stakeholders, generating sales and opportunities from outside your existing circle of contacts, improving the profile and credibility of your senior team, attracting talented team members and suppliers, gaining support from key stakeholders for initiatives, winning awards, raising your price points and the value of your business, protecting your reputation at a time of crisis and encouraging people to believe in your advertising. You will feel the difference if PR is working, but to achieve these positive impacts takes time. PR is a slow-burn process and, in the case of publicity, needs to be targeted at the right media and read by your ideal audiences with the right messaging over a sustained period.

There is a huge focus now in the PR industry to set clear objectives, and then measure the PR campaign against them. This is a paradigm shift away from the old ways of focusing on outputs and tactics like generating publicity, which can just result in scattergun press releases being greeted with the sound of a thousand delete buttons. The key now is to provide laser focus to PR campaigns' objectives.

Sam Black's seminal book references some of the deadly sins of PR, which still ring true:[28]

- **Functional myopia.** We don't appreciate the full scope of the important contribution PR can make to good management.

- **Faucet philosophy.** We turn on PR only when we need it.

- **Good news delusion.** We only believe in public information if it reflects positively and favourably upon us.

- **The one-shot communication tick.** We believe communication is something that only needs to happen once. Eg 'We don't understand why you accuse us of not communicating – the issue was mentioned in our last annual report.'

- **The shadow delusion.** We believe that we can keep a low profile or make our company invisible whenever we choose.

The difference between PR and advertising

PR and advertising both try to influence behaviour and attitudes, but PR's influence is earned whereas advertising's is paid for. PR, in the form of publicity, has to go through a third party, a journalist, before it is published on news pages as editorial for free.

A PR consultant's work is to convince reporters to write about their clients through the strength of a news release or pitch. As a result, editorial is generally independent, credible and has a high acceptance of message with readers. PR messaging tends to be more in depth than advertising with a long-term aim to influence attitudes. Advertising is more sales driven and short term.

PR is not controlled, while advertising is. This lack of control can expose an organisation to negative coverage if the reporter or host publication has a political bias or an axe to grind. In this case, the PR consultant has to be alert to which media are hostile. And critically, the consultant can really make a difference by directly engaging the media outlet to correct any inaccuracy and ensure balanced reporting. This does not need to be confrontational or nasty – rather robust and in a spirit of understanding and constructive cooperation. Reporters usually respect a PR consultant who communicates with them and helps them get their facts right.

Key points

- Every organisation, no matter how large or small, ultimately depends on its reputation for survival and success.

- PR works best when the CEO or founder believes in it and thrusts it to the centre of the business.

- PR is more than a tactical tool used purely to communicate information or add gloss; it is integral to the business's strategic development process.

- PR requires clear objectives and methods of measuring from the outset.

- PR can create sales and opportunities but cannot work in a vacuum. Businesses must proactively harvest the profile PR creates.

- PR can help position your company for sale, increase its value and attract investors. But it is a slow-burn process.

- The benefits of PR cannot be measured in outputs like media coverage. Impact is measured on whether it influences and changes stakeholder attitudes and behaviour.

- PR is different to advertising. It is independent and not paid for. Coverage is not controlled or guaranteed but carries a high acceptance of message.

3
Brand Ethos And Unique Selling Points

The starting point for a PR campaign is the company brand. The brand or ethos is the soul of the company, the life source from which PR messaging grows.

Too often, companies do not truly understand how to harness or communicate their brand. Executives do not think it matters or it is PR puff or a flashy logo. But it is so much more.

Find your higher purpose

A brand at its best will inspire an ethos and an attitude. It often comes from the founder or owner – what is motivating them? It is usually much more than simply what the business does to make a living. There will be passion, drive and determination behind it, and that is what you want to dig into. The best brands are built around a higher purpose that drives the business – something that shows that the business is more than what it does.

Perhaps you have a will to address a big problem. In maritime, there are massive issues to throw your brand weight behind, such as tackling GHG emissions and pollution of the oceans. Perhaps you have a product or service that makes people safer at sea. The point is that if you can find a higher purpose and make it part of your brand, it can become a philosophy that is so contagious, so powerful, it snaps people out of their stupor and inspires them.

If you are truly making a positive difference, think how that could inspire your clients, workforce and stakeholders to believe in you and become passionate about your business. The best communications always put people first – show you are sensitive to and care about your team and clients. If you fail to prioritise people in your business communications, you will almost certainly come unstuck.

Once you have a clear idea what you stand for, you can start telling your stories with this ethos shining through. You want to find the blood-and-thunder stories in your company – the triumphs and adversities overcome. This is when the fire in your belly – your authentic company ethos – can really come alive.

During a 1997 presentation at Apple, Steve Jobs advised that crystal clarity on brand values is essential to be heard in a complicated, noisy marketplace: 'We're not going to get the chance to get people to remember much about us. No company is. So we have to be really clear on what we want them to know about us.'[29]

Apple famously created the 'think different' marketing campaign, championing rebels and misfits like John Lennon, Mohammed Ali and Mahatma Gandhi. Apple saw genius in these and any people who think they can change the world, as they are the ones who tend to do so. This edgy, uplifting campaign was about more than Apple products; it inspired people with Apple's disruptive, world-changing entrepreneurial attitude.

Richard Branson is another passionate believer in authentic marketing, lamenting the fact that: 'Too many companies want their brands to reflect some idealized, perfected image of themselves. Consequently, their brands acquire no texture, no character.'[30] His company Virgin stands for fun, adventure, customer service, entrepreneurship, being outlandish. That is the power of a strong brand – it communicates an outlook.

When you look around the marketplace, how often do you see business owners and CEOs talking earnestly about having reliability or integrity? While this is laudable, it has no power. These are the values most business owners would trot out without thought – vapid niceties which do not inspire. You need to think about what makes you *different*. What makes you stand out? What is true to your character? What is your higher purpose? What is the big change you want to see in the world or the maritime industry?

CASE STUDY – CAMMELL LAIRD

One of the most powerful examples of an ethos I have witnessed was from John Syvret, the entrepreneur who revived the Merseyside shipbuilder **Cammell Laird**, which became a Polaris client for over ten years. It was a real buzz to promote such a passionate vision.

I remember John pointing out of his window to the shipyard and saying the company could generate work for people of all abilities and skillsets. He often said what motivated him was creating jobs for the families of Birkenhead, particularly for young apprentices. A former apprentice himself, he could speak with authority and would say that an apprenticeship at Lairds gave young men and women pride; they could sit at the family dinner table and show they had a responsible career, a skill and a future with an iconic business.

When the Lairds team spoke about their desire to revive the company, it was unbelievably powerful. Stories poured out of the yard, forging an incredible bond and camaraderie. As someone who comes from Merseyside, I found this attitude hugely motivating as a contractor. I can honestly say it helped to get me out of bed in the morning, knowing that my new PR firm was helping to support this real and meaningful endeavour. In my own small way, I could positively improve my home city.

I know many others who worked for Lairds felt similarly – the brand ethos was contagious and powerful and generated huge goodwill and political support. From this ethos, other positive messages flowed, such as recalibrating heavily depleted engineering skills locally and nationally. It encouraged young people to choose maritime as a career, with all the opportunities and excitement that come with a global industry.

But this was about something more than what the company did. Yes, Cammell Laird was excellent at building and repairing ships, but the higher purpose was in the economic and societal good it was doing.

The results of this higher purpose speak for themselves. In the 13 years Polaris worked with Cammell Laird, the media loved reporting on the renaissance of the business, and organisations were falling over themselves to hand out awards. Lairds won awards with the Liverpool Echo, North West Insider, BusinessDesk.com, Wirral Chamber and Mersey Maritime, and John Syvret was awarded a CBE. And crucially, the business flowed in with big Ministry of Defence contracts, the likes of the Royal Fleet Auxiliary and Aircraft Carrier Alliance motivated to invest in skills in an economically deprived area.

The campaign culminated in the awarding in 2015 of the contract to build the RRS Sir David Attenborough polar research vessel, the biggest commercial shipbuilding project in Britain for 30 years. The greatness that the team aspired to, drawing on the immense achievements of the company's shipbuilding past, had been equalled. These were momentous times which drew national and international attention. Quite something for a business that had seen its gates closed in 2000. The grit, spirit and vision of the founder helped forge a brand ethos that dragged the business back into the big time. And while not every business is as big as Lairds or has an iconic heritage the approach is the same.

It can sometimes take time for businesses to find their higher purpose. But if you are searching for ways to build an ethos, look at the United Nations 17 Sustainable Development Goals.[31] It is fascinating to see how these are being adopted at the highest level in the maritime industry by the likes of Lloyd's Register and Fugro, and even trade fairs like Nor-Shipping in Oslo.

SUSTAINABLE DEVELOPMENT G⚙ALS

See www.un.org/sustainabledevelopment for more information on the UN Sustainable Development Goals.

The content of this publication has not been approved by the United Nations and does not reflect the views of the United Nations or its officials or Member States.

CASE STUDY – LLOYD'S REGISTER

Lloyd's Register (LR) is one of the most respected names in maritime. An £868m turnover classification society owned by the Lloyd's Register Foundation, a UK charity, LR has a strong ethos that is powerfully communicated, particularly in forums like its annual report.

Writing in the 2018/19 report entitled 'Reaching New Heights for a Safer World',[32] LR chairman Thomas Thune Andersen emphasised the brand's higher purpose in his opening statement.

'Throughout change and volatility, our purpose remains resolute – working together for a safer world. LR's expertise across safety, security and sustainability, combined with the work of the Foundation, is focussed on making a positive impact on society within a purpose-driven business model for the 21st century. Safety underpins all that we do and remains a priority for the board, executive team and colleagues. The board is increasing its focus on diversity and inclusion and I am pleased to report progress towards the closing of the gender pay gap and the deployment of LR's new Diversity and Inclusion Programme across all leadership teams this year.

'In the two years since LR became a signatory to the United Nations Global Compact (UNGC), the guardian of the UN Sustainable Development Goals (SDGs) and the world's largest corporate responsibility initiative, I am delighted to witness the progress being made. This includes the launch of the UNGC's Ocean Opportunities, Global Goals report[33] on the role of business for a healthy, productive and well-governed ocean and our signatory to its Sustainable Ocean Principles covering climate change, ocean health and productivity; governance and engagement; and data and transparency. Our emphasis on ocean sustainability is reinforced in our work supporting customers to prepare to meet the obligations of the IMO's 2050 GHG reduction target with further work on zero-emission vessels in partnership with the Global Maritime Forum.'

(Details used with kind permission of Kate Delahunty, Corporate Affairs Director, Lloyd's Register.)

CASE STUDY – FUGRO

Another brand finding a match and vehicle for its ethos in the SDGs is **Fugro**, the Netherlands-based engineering company. When asked how Fugro aims to support a safer and more sustainable world, Mark Heine, its Chairman and CEO, said:

'We are experts in understanding the risks of overusing the earth. We provide information about the earth and structures built upon it to help design, build and operate our client's assets in a safe, sustainable manner. Also, in a company that gets half of its revenue from the oil and gas industry but is now also doing 50 per cent of its activities in offshore wind, infrastructure and nautical, climate change is a topic of daily discussion. Hydrography plays an increasingly large role for Fugro because of climate change as we map coastlines and coastal zones to learn more about tsunami hazards or rising sea levels.

'Much of Fugro's land business has a direct impact on sustainable infrastructure development. Fugro is increasingly involved in projects that map and mitigate the

51

impact of climate change. Growth in renewable energy is strong and has a global reach. We've chosen five SDGs... we now need to work towards meeting these goals.

'Our expertise has always contributed to our purpose by creating a safe, liveable and sustainable world.'

(Details used with kind permission of Edward Legierse, Director Corporate Strategy and Communication, Fugro.)

CASE STUDY – NOR-SHIPPING

On its website, **Nor-Shipping** reports that its event programme tailors activity to address numerous SDGs, with special focus on gender equality (SDG 5), climate action (SDG 13), life below water (SDG 14) and partnerships for the goals (SDG 17). Here's an excerpt from the Nor-Shipping website:

The Nor-Shipping Principles:

Nor-Shipping has released the very first 'Nor-Shipping Principles',[34] detailing both a code of conduct for exhibitors and participants and its commitment to supporting, and encouraging others to support, key UN SDGs.

Sustainable Ocean Principles:

Nor-Shipping has signed the Sustainable Ocean Principles and commits to ensure that material ocean-related risks and opportunities are integrated in corporate strategy, risk management and reporting.

The Blue Economy hall:

Nor-Shipping 2019 devoted an entire hall to the theme of Blue Economy. This hall focused on showcasing and accelerating innovations and businesses that build commercial value in the ocean space, while safeguarding the environment and ensuring the sustainable use of resources. This is the world's first dedicated commercial platform for maritime opportunities supporting the SDGs, showcasing tomorrow's business solutions today. Focus areas for the Blue Economy hall were based on the DNV opportunity report 'Sustainable Development Goals – Exploring Maritime Opportunities – 2016'.[35]

(Details used with kind permission of Christina Dupré Roos, Partner and Press Relations Manager, Nor-Shipping.)

I'm sure you're getting a feel for how the maritime industry is evolving its branding to the challenges facing the industry and the world. Perhaps you can use the UN SDGs to focus your communications and brand voice?

A good method for reviewing your brand is to undertake a market analysis of competitors to establish their brand identity, tone of voice and what they stand for, and see how you can better differentiate yourself. You can also survey your staff, suppliers and contractors and ask them what they think your company stands for.

From here, you can start to build your brand ethos, guidelines and company vision – mission statement and values. Bigger companies tend to concentrate on the mission statement and values, but I advise you to be careful of these becoming too idealised. A true brand is authentic and has a clear, distinctive voice when it speaks across all PR and marketing materials. And more importantly, your founders, team and contractors live and embody the brand outlook. That enthusiasm is so infectious, it is passed on to customers and clients.

Think of ethos as a compass – if you feel fed up with something or team members seem flat and their eyes are glazed over, the ethos is there to inspire and remind you and your team why you are doing this. It needs to have that power to inspire and challenge.

With Polaris, for example, the positivity injected into the brand around 'passion' lives in the team. Passion sets a high bar for us to aspire to. I can turn to it when searching for motivation and energy.

During the Covid pandemic, we ran a mini #think-passion social media campaign celebrating the work of creatives who have inspired us and made a huge impact on so many people's lives through their imagination and raw passion – figures like Charles Dickens, Charlotte Bronte, Robert Smith and Muddy Waters. It reminded the team what passion can achieve. It also said to me that caring and standards must be central to what we do.

As a small business owner, you need to stand out for trying your absolute best for your clients. Otherwise, what is the point?

A final word on ethos – it may sound obvious, but caring for your people and customers must be central to your ethos and how you communicate. Time and again, business owners and CEOs go wrong in communications when they misjudge people's reaction and seem self-interested, cold, insensitive. Always think about the human response first.

In an age of social media, everyone has a voice. If you are tone deaf to an issue and how people feel, it can blow up badly in your face, causing serious reputational harm.

TIP

A good strapline captures your ethos with energy and intent. The best are positive, short and memorable.

Here are some famous examples:

- Flying in the face of ordinary – Virgin Atlantic
- Forever Cunard – Cunard Line's 175th anniversary slogan
- Your promise. Delivered – Maersk
- Your potential, our passion – Microsoft
- The ultimate driving machine – BMW
- Think different – Apple
- The voice of business – The CBI
- Connecting people – Nokia

Unique selling points

While discovering the ethos of your company, you can work on its unique selling points (USPs). It is important to embed the benefits of using your company and products in your PR rather than simply focusing on the technical side, as it is the benefits that are more likely to hook in the customer. Also, managers you deal with may need to 'sell' you and your company to their boss to get a deal over the line, so being able to articulate the benefits you bring is a huge help to them, too. Do the spadework for them: have the USPs ready so they jump off the page in a cluttered market space.

Some of the best meetings I have had with clients come from the search for a company's USPs. I have seen teams sparking off each other as they start to articulate a deep purpose within themselves that they may not have properly crystallised before.

Think of how Elon Musk disrupted the car market with Tesla. What makes Tesla stand out is how astonishingly innovative the cars are compared to other vehicles. Tesla is excellent at creating lots of touch points, emphasising its USPs to prospective buyers. You can do the same, harnessing an array of communications materials covering publicity, social media, e-newsletters, YouTube and brochures.

CASE STUDY – GRIFFON

The famous Southampton hovercraft maker **Griffon Hoverwork**, which has been at the forefront of making hovercrafts since they were first conceived, has superb USPs. Today, the company has hovercrafts in more than 40 countries.

Working with its gregarious Marketing and Sales Director Nick MacLeod-Ash, Polaris has been able to highlight these USPs. Polaris was engaged to promote the global launch of Griffon's 995ED model at Latin America's premier naval and maritime exhibition ExpoNaval in Valparaiso, Chile, the news release reporting that hovercraft can go places ordinary boats cannot.

Nick said, 'Hovercrafts are extremely effective in flood and disaster roles where search and rescue using conventional patrol boats and rigid inflatable boats (RIBs) can be extremely difficult. The hovercraft like the 995ED can operate brilliantly in shallow water, rivers and over ice, weed and mud. In these cases, boats cannot navigate the conditions and helicopters are extremely expensive and have limited passenger capacity and payload. The 995ED, on the other hand, can travel over almost any surface, including debris, which is becoming a bigger problem with increased flooding and tsunami events.'

(Details used with kind permission of Nicholas MacLeod-Ash, Marketing and Sales Director, Griffon Hoverwork Ltd.)

CASE STUDY – OMAN DRYDOCK

Another Polaris client with powerful USPs is the Middle East shipyard **Oman Drydock**. I remember vividly its then Marketing Director Johnny Woo pointing out a map in his Muscat office one beautiful evening. He showed how the shipyard's location in Duqm meant that vessels did not have to navigate one of the most crowded and treacherous shipping lanes in the world, the Strait of Hormuz, frequently a flashpoint for mine laying and tensions with Iran, to reach shipyards in Dubai or Qatar.

As the then Deputy CEO Dr Ahmed Al Abri said in a press release, 'Our geographical position is one of our key USPs. The convenience we can offer means ship owners can save time and money by not having to deviate course through the Strait of Hormuz. Furthermore, we offer the ideal climate for painting and blasting, which other shipyards in the Gulf cannot match.'

CASE STUDY – JAMES TROOP

Closer to home, Polaris worked with the famous Liverpool ship engine company **James Troop**. A representative of the company told us they had moved to new premises in Runcorn so they could 'put their customer first'. The new location enabled ease of access to the motorway and connections so the team could move with maximum efficiency to support its clients.

From here, a powerfully authentic PR message and ethos shone out. James Troop is a dedicated, selfless company, one of the virtues that had enabled it to trade successfully for 150 years.

(Details used with kind permission of Robert Pollock, Managing Director (Operations), James Troop and Co Ltd.)

CASE STUDY – ISLE OF MAN SHIP REGISTRY

Over the water in the Irish Sea, the **Isle of Man Ship Registry (IOMSR)** prides itself on being a high-quality flag state of choice that regularly features at the top of the Paris Whitelist, which ranks flag states by performance. The IOMSR wanted to emphasise its commitment to safety and care for seafarers, a big responsibility with nearly half of shipping under the Red Ensign – around 10,000 seafarers – now covered by the IOMSR flag.

The Director Cameron Mitchell, a former seafarer himself, told me he passionately wanted to do something to help seafarers combat the isolation many feel in the wilderness of the sea. This had been brought into sharp focus by the apparent suicide of a seafarer on an IOMSR flagged ship. As a result, in partnership with tech company Tapiit Live, the registry launched the first seafarer welfare app created by a flag state called 'Crew Matters'.

The messaging in the press release and social media underlined how genuine this care for seafarers was, drawing on Cameron's experience at sea for seventeen years. IOMSR did not just talk about crew welfare, it actually went out and did something about it. As well as being a unique offering, the welfare app says a lot about the outlook of the registry and what makes it tick.

(Details used with kind permission of Cameron Mitchell, Director, Isle of Man Ship Registry.)

CASE STUDY – ROXTEC

Roxtec is a large international manufacturer of safety seals used extensively in the maritime and offshore sectors. The company wants its seals to be known for protecting people, buildings and assets. The products are incredibly robust and testing in Sweden is meticulous, but it is the benefits of the product the company wants to highlight, not just the technical quality.

Another great message from Roxtec is its global reach with offices all over the world, providing in-country engineering expertise. This is so important when maritime and offshore projects can involve numerous countries and interlocking supply chains.

These are the types of messages which give you a competitive edge and character and are central to building a strong brand.

One way to focus on your ethos and USPs is to produce a set of brand guidelines with your PR team. This can capture what your brand stands for and what your voice should sound like in marketing and PR materials, together with clear guidance on how your logo and identity will be used. Again, it is helpful if you can benchmark yourself against competitors. A brand consultant can help you understand what makes you different.

Once you have your brand and your USPs and you know what you stand for, you have a bedrock on which to build a communications plan. And that is what we will focus on in the next chapter.

Key points

- Brand is the starting point from which PR and communications messaging grows.

- Look at what motivates your company's founder or owners. Brands require authentic character and texture, so avoid being bland or idealised – you will not stand out.

- Having a higher purpose is contagious – you are more than what you do.

- Many companies across the maritime sector are adopting the UN's SDGs to underpin ethos.

- Work on your USPs and use them consistently across PR and marketing.

- Have USPs ready for people to use internally. You cannot rely on middle managers to know how to sell you to their boss to secure your deal.

4
Building A Communications Plan

A carefully considered communications plan is critical to the success of your PR campaign. Everyone who is involved with the marketing and communications of your business needs to understand your plan. Whether yours is a large or small business or organisation, your plan will help crystallise your objectives, describe how you are going to achieve them and explain how you will evaluate impact and progress.

Every good plan starts with a clear brief and an agreement about what success looks like. Campaign assessment can change without warning, leading to uncomfortable meetings where managers introduce new criteria that were not in the original proposal or discussed in review meetings. A communications plan can stop this kind of situation emerging, preventing goal posts being moved by keeping everyone focused. And when a new management team comes in, it provides them with a template to adapt the plan to their outlook.

When you begin building your plan, it is helpful to let your PR consultant read your wider business strategies and understand what the board wishes to achieve. Your PR consultant should have a firm grasp of the strengths, weaknesses, opportunities and threats (SWOT) facing the company from your SWOT analysis, as well as an understanding of the political, economic, social, technological and legal environment in which you operate. It is better to be frank and open on this, however sensitive. If you are concerned about confidentiality, ensure there is a contract in place.

How to choose a PR consultant

A credible PR firm should be a member of an industry body such as the CIPR. From here, it can offer its standard contract, terms and conditions, and provide a code of conduct. This clearly sets out confidentiality clauses and prevents unprofessional conduct.

But do be aware that PR as an industry can be undermined by people claiming to be experienced professionals without any formal training or industry body membership. Look for a National Council for the Training of Journalists (NCTJ) qualification and experience of working in newspapers or reputable trade media publications if a PR consultant says they have a journalism background.

For PR professionals more broadly, look for certification of a PR degree as well as membership of the CIPR or the Public Relations and Communications Association (PRCA). Look also for examples of commitment to training, and ensure your advisers are bound by a professional code of conduct.

Sharing information and building trust with your communications advisers is essential. A good adviser needs to hear the heartbeat of your organisation and be the person you turn to when things go wrong as well as right, so rapport is crucial before developing key foundations like the communications plan.

Communications plan structure

A communications plan needs to include:

- Strategy purpose
- Mission and vision
- SMART objectives
- Audiences
- Messaging
- Channels

- Team and budget

- Risks and mitigation

- Evaluation

The final two points will be covered in chapters yet to come. For now, let's look in more detail at strategy purpose down to team and budget.

Strategy purpose

What exactly is strategy purpose? If you, for example, want the aim of the plan to be to provide a written reference document to focus the objectives of the communications campaign during the next twelve months, you will set out what the campaign is designed to achieve, who it is aimed at, where it will reach, when communications events are planned and how they will be delivered. You will then detail which people and businesses will manage and implement the campaign, which communications channels will be deployed, what the risks are that it poses, what resources are required, and detail how it can be measured.

Mission and vision

Here, you want to lay out the communication plan's mission and vision. You may want it to help the company become recognised as, for example:

- One of the UK's most innovative companies in your niche, serving the global maritime industry while building on your standards as a British brand.

- A business which contributes substantially to the local/regional and UK maritime industry.

- A business where people feel valued and are passionate about working with you.

- A business which supports the development of skills in young people.

- A business where clients and stakeholders feel valued and motivated and are passionate about supporting you.

SMART objectives

Your communications plan needs to acknowledge and support the business plan's SMART – Smart, Measurable, Achievable, Realistic and Timely – objectives, while at the business end of the communications plan are the SMART PR objectives. When you're working these out, be fair to the process, and be clear where the company is now from a communications perspective. What is your starting position?

Ask yourself these kinds of questions:

- What is the company's current profile?

- How are we known, what is our reputation?

- Are we seen to be growing in popularity and have momentum?

- What do we invest in PR? Who are the team driving our PR?

- What is our relationship with the media?

- What is our presence on social media?

- How well known is our front person? Are they seen as a credible expert? Do they appear in the media and publish thought-leadership articles?

- Do we expect the PR campaign to generate direct sales or create the right awareness and messages to support our sales team?

- Are we already undertaking marketing activities that PR can support?

From here, you can set your SMART PR objectives accordingly, for example:

- Raise global awareness of our company, leaders and products.

- Engage and harness support from our clients and stakeholders in our publicity and social media.

- Raise awareness of key messages explaining our USPs, commitment to inspiring young people and decarbonisation.

- Drive traffic to our website for rich content.

- Generate twenty leads each year from PR activities.

- Apply for five industry awards.

- Generate PR before and during trade fairs.

Remember to keep a dynamic eye on your objectives and ensure you are flexible to change so the PR campaign can respond to industry events and new opportunities. Being SMART, these objectives always build in time for performance reviews.

Audiences

Be clear about who you want to reach with your PR activity and how you will tailor the messaging to them. If you try to please everyone, it will not work.

You may have different messages for different audiences and media. For example, your regional media may focus on economics and jobs in the local area, the national press may focus on your exports drive, and the maritime media may look more at the benefits of your services and products.

Example audiences:

- **Internal:** workforce, board, trade union, shareholders

- **External:** customers (existing, lapsed and potential), suppliers, the media, local and national government/politicians, trade associations, local community (relevant businesses and charities, schools, colleges, universities, prospective employees and their families and friends), competitors

Messaging

Define messaging in line with your target audiences, brand ethos and USPs. For example:

People and skills: One of the great selling points of maritime is the vast array of employment opportunities it provides across white- and blue-collar skills, from engineering to finance to marketing. If you are employing apprentices in disciplines where there is a skills gap, promote this as a commercial asset and something that requires support from politicians and policy makers. You can also emphasise your company's commitment to equality of opportunity, providing structured training for people of all ages to upskill. Perhaps report your support for the IMO's Women in Maritime gender programme and Maritime UK's Women in Maritime programme to address gender imbalance in the industry, as well as the wider Diversity in Maritime programme supporting Gay Pride and ethnic minorities – giving examples of your support in action.

Decarbonisation: This is a red-hot issue to have a voice on. Think about how you can support the IMO's 2050 GHG emissions target. Show what you are doing to help ships become greener and your maritime clients meet the GHG targets. Adopt the UN SDGs, join the Getting to Zero Coalition and support its work. Acknowledge the Poseidon Principles. Be vocal on relevant awareness days like World Ocean Day, World Environment Day or Clean Air Day.

Digitisation: This is the other prime issue driving change in maritime. What is your position? How are you embracing technology to adapt and improve your operations and help your customers?

Value: Money matters. Think about how your company provides clients with value. Polaris client Roxtec deploys PR to emphasise how durable and easy-to-install its seals are, slashing down on costly repairs and engineering time.

Economic importance: This is a big message. Here, you can emphasise the contribution your company makes as a job and wealth creator, sustaining employment and suppliers, and injecting cash into the local economy and UK Treasury. These messages have real resonance with stakeholders.

UK maritime industry: Whether your business is a small/medium-sized enterprise or corporate, align your communications to all the work being done to support the UK maritime industry. This will strengthen your stature, make you better known, and help with awareness and networking.

Nationally, the Maritime UK industry body is driving awareness of the sector through the network of regional maritime clusters, as well as big events such as London International Shipping Week and its own awards ceremony. This activity supports the Government's Maritime 2050 manifesto. Position yourself in support of this body to show you are an influencer in the sector.

Entrepreneurship: Embedding an entrepreneurial culture in your messaging gives you an edge. It aligns you to the 'start small, dream big' attitude of those who have made it in business from small beginnings, which is inspiring.

Having an entrepreneurial outlook can work in a big business as well. Being entrepreneurial shows your team and stakeholders you are alive to change, willing to diversify and adapt, and a problem solver.

Channels

This is the place to identify the channels you will use to reach your different audiences. For example:

- Lobbying
- Media
- Social media
- Site visits

- Membership bodies

- Brochures

- Company films

- Advertising
  Example: A company has an advertising budget of £40,000 a year for the international maritime press. It expects this to help it reach 100,000–200,000 readers a month in print and appear at publisher events and webinars. The design of the advert is changed every six months.

- Company newsletters
  Example: A company issues a bi-monthly internal newsletter from the CEO for staff. This document is a mix of soft and hard news from around the business, giving a detailed account of how the business is performing. The company produces a quarterly e-newsletter aimed at customers and stakeholders. A round-up of positive news such as new deals, investments and appointments, it is distributed worldwide via email and social media.

- Awards
  Example: A company has a track record of winning high-profile awards which are effective endorsements of key messages and stakeholder engagement. It has a case for applying for national awards such as *Lloyd's List* and the Queen's Award for Enterprise as well as regional awards.

- Trade fairs
  Example: A company has a budget of £200,000 for trade fairs and plans to exhibit in the UK Pavilion at SMM in Hamburg, Posidonia in Greece, Nor-Shipping in Oslo, Marintec in Shanghai, as well as Seawork in Southampton and Offshore Oil and Gas in Aberdeen. The PR campaign needs to dovetail with the sales team to support its leads and conversion objectives.

Team and budgets

This section of the plan is the place to include information about the people who will undertake the work and the total budget available. Identify who is responsible for managing press and other communication activities. I would advise that the CEO or MD has a close overseeing role on this, together with an in-house marketing team.

It is important to factor in total costs such as executive time for managing the PR campaign and the cost of holding events and attending awards ceremonies.

TIP

Companies should look to invest 5–10 per cent of their turnover into marketing and PR.

We will cover risks in Chapter 8, and evaluation will be covered in detail in the next chapter.

Key points

- A communications plan is critical to the success of your PR campaigns.

- Before building your plan, let your PR consultant read your wider business strategies.

- Look for an NCTJ qualification and experience of working in newspapers or trade media if a PR consultant says they have a journalism background.

- For other PR professionals, look for a PR degree and membership of the CIPR or the PRCA.

- A good PR adviser needs to hear the heartbeat of your organisation and be the person you turn to, whether things are going wrong or right.

- When you come to craft your communications plan, make sure it includes:

  - Strategy purpose

  - Mission and vision

  - SMART objectives

  - Audiences

  - Messaging

  - Channels

  - Team and budget

  - Risks and mitigation

  - Evaluation

5
Evaluation Methods

Evaluating PR campaigns is one of the hottest topics in PR. What I provide here is an introduction to
a big debate.

Evaluation has been seen as a weakness of the PR
industry. Too often, PR consultants who pride themselves on their storytelling *do not* tell the story of the
impact of the campaign from the data and intelligence
they have collected. Evaluation can be seen as dull and
esoteric, when it is actually one of the most important
elements of any campaign.

Evaluation is the business end of the campaign
where you track progress in line with your communications plan objectives. The CEO and the PR team
work together to understand how the campaign will

be measured – it is basic good management and will help in setting the communications plan objectives in the first place.

You want to understand what you are achieving, what the return on investment (ROI) is and what you do with the findings. This final point is critical because one of the prime benefits of evaluation is to adapt and improve the campaign.

It is worth recognising how nuanced PR has become beyond the realm of media relations. The landscape has changed so much, with PR opportunities abundant on owned media (company websites, blogs and social media) as well as paid-for promotion on channels like LinkedIn and mainstream media. This has led to a new measurement definition called paid, earned, shared and owned (PESO).

The concept of PESO gained recognition when it was used by Gini Dietrich in her 2014 book *Spin Sucks*.[36] PESO is applied to integrated marketing campaigns and examines the strengths and weaknesses of media types:

- **Paid:** Traditional mainstream media advertising, social media adverts/sponsorship, pay per click, brand ambassadors.

- **Earned:** Coverage earned usually generated by a press release or PR pitch to mainstream independent media, bloggers or industry commentators.

- **Shared:** The engagements, comments and shares your content receives, usually online through social media. (Owned, earned and paid media can all turn into shared media.)

- **Owned:** The editorial content and messages your company writes, publishes and controls through your own channels such as website, social media, e-newsletters, brochures, films, podcasts, white papers and blogs.

This table shows the relative benefits and drawbacks of the different types of media.[37]

	Trust	Scale	Cost	Predictability
Paid	Low	High	High	Yes
Earned	High	Medium	Low to medium	No
Shared	High	Low	Low	No
Owned	Low to medium	Low	Low to medium	Yes

As well as being sober about the impacts of different types of media, you will also need to be realistic about what can be achieved when you evaluate your campaign, hence evaluation informing the creation of the objectives. Ensure you do not overestimate PR by either setting impractical coverage expectations or expecting it to change highly entrenched views.

How to start the evaluation process

To start the evaluation process, I advise following the excellent work of the Association for Measurement and Evaluation of Communication (AMEC), which is driving PR measurement techniques.[38] It really is worth taking time to explore the AMEC website for the latest commentary, case studies and in-depth reports on the field of evaluation.

To deliver effectiveness, AMEC advises you need to see outputs, out-takes, outcomes as a chain – one leads to the next, and together they help to deliver the desired impact.

- **Outputs** are when media cuttings, folders or social media reports are produced.

- **Out-takes** take place after a PR campaign has been in place for some time, when people start to understand and remember your messaging.

- **Outcomes** arrive when the understanding grows into trust and people change their attitudes or behaviour because of the PR activities.

- **Impact** is the ultimate follow-on result that is related to objectives your communications achieved or contributed to.

AMEC has put together the following table to further explain outputs, out-takes, outcomes and impact.[39]

Outputs	Out-takes	Outcomes	Impact
Outputs include:	... are your target audience's initial responses and reactions to your communications. These may be interim steps towards your objectives, not necessarily achievement of your objectives. Out-takes may include evidence of:	... of the effect that your communication has on your target audiences that align to your objectives. Examples of outcomes of communication include:	... is the ultimate follow-on results related to your objectives which your communication achieved or contributed to. Impact can include:
Publicity information	Audience attention, eg unique visitors, views, click throughs	Learning/knowledge, eg through survey or interview data, quizzes or tests	Reputation improvement recognised as an intangible asset
Websites, blogs, partnerships or supplements	Awareness, eg recall	Trust, eg increased trust in surveys	Relationships established or improved also recognised as an intangible asset by the international integrated reporting council

(Continued)

Cont.

Outputs	Out-takes	Outcomes	Impact
Events held	Understanding, eg comments	Preference, eg in surveys or social media comment	Reaching targets, eg sales revenue, fundraising or membership targets, health campaign targets such as reduced smoking
Sponsorships launched	Interest and liking, eg likes, follows, shares, retweets	Intention, eg through surveys, enquiries, trialling or registration	Increased staff loyalty or retention, eg reduced staff turnover and recruitment costs
	Engagement, eg return visits, positive comments, subscribing	Attitude change through surveys or interview data	Organisational change, eg insights to inform future strategy, realignment of policies to stakeholders
		Complying behaviour, eg sales, donations, driving safely, voting	Social change, eg improved health and well being or increased access to information
		Advocacy, eg endorsements in online comments	

Use these measurements to evaluate how you are meeting your communications plan objectives. Generally, if you are experiencing the benefits and outcomes/impacts of PR, which can include winning awards, stakeholders engaging with you personally and supporting you in difficult times, greater interest in your business from the media with increased take up of your press releases and more requests for interview and comment, increase in the value of your business and your price points, approaches to speak at industry events and join committees, proactive feedback on your publicity from stakeholders, new business leads, you are getting it right.

Outputs – publicity

Here, the PR consultancy or press office can submit data on how many press releases have been issued and what coverage they have generated. At Polaris, we upload all media coverage using the Coverage-Book software. This crunches the readership of print and online coverage, calculating shares on Twitter and Facebook, but not LinkedIn. It can be accessed in real time via a permanent link as it is updated.

Print readership is calculated by the number of readers per copy. The industry standard is to multiple the circulation by between 2.5 and 4 readers – meaning for each copy sold, estimate that up to four people will read it.

Out-takes/outcomes/impact – publicity

The quantity of coverage and the advertising value equivalent (AVE) of copy are blunt instruments for measuring the impact of a PR campaign. Coverage can, after all, include negative stories. Moreover, in terms of readership, while you may hit high numbers in the maritime press, you may actually be reaching many of the same people via so-called 'cross reading'.

For example, some people who read *TradeWinds* are also reading *Lloyd's List*. As a result, audience figures, while a useful barometer, are also an inexact science.

The benefits of PR are not in the AVE, but in what the PR achieves in influencing attitudes, opinion and behaviour. PR is different to advertising; it has the impact of impartiality because a journalist has independently decided to run the story for free. It is the quality of the coverage that counts most. And this is what you need to capture and report back.

Is the company appearing in titles read by your target audiences? Is the messaging aligned to your communications plan objectives? Keep in mind that one article or feature interview in, say, the *Financial Times*, *Ship Repair Journal* or *TradeWinds* could be more valuable to your company than numerous articles in local press if it reaches more of your target audience.

TIP

A single article or particular story may have a disproportionate impact on stakeholder attitudes.

Think of Princess Diana and the Martin Bashir interview – Diana generated huge volumes of coverage, but that one interview and the story it revealed had more impact than countless other reports. The more recent Duke and Duchess of Sussex interview with Oprah Winfrey is a similar example of a single high-impact interview.

Meanwhile, when the UK Prime Minister's then Chief of Staff Dominic Cummings broke the lockdown rules by visiting his family in the North of England during the Covid pandemic, coverage around this story had a big negative effect on the government's credibility and the authority of its 'stay at home' message. The outcome and impact, although powerful in influencing attitudes, were opposite to what the government's communications team was trying to achieve.

As I am sure you can see, it is essential to assess media coverage in the right way. Do not look solely at volume and high readership rates; assess impact, too.

In terms of quality analysis, you could use a points-based system for marking each piece of coverage, starting with the importance of the publication it appears in, then giving marks for inclusion of a product, picture or senior leader you want to position as a key person of influence 'frontperson'.[40] How big is the report? Is it on the stronger right-hand page in print or is it positioned prominently on a news website or e-newsletter? Does it include your key messages and any independent commentary on your status in the sector? Is that commentary positive or negative?

If a prime outcome and impact of your PR is to change attitudes and behaviours and improve your reputation, it is worth finding out what people think. You can employ a third party to undertake surveys or focus groups for you. The cost of this has reduced considerably in recent times, but you may feel it is a lot of effort to hold a stakeholder focus group, so why not start with a short survey via a trade body? Alternatively, you can use www.surveymonkey.com, which provides free survey templates and guides to analysing results.

If these tools reveal useful information about the out-takes, outcomes and impact of your PR campaign, you could then employ the services of a professional polling body. The results may not always make comfortable reading, but acting on them may make you more profitable if you understand your customer better.

In politics, polling is constant, but it's much less common in business, particularly in the maritime sector. For example, the former Scottish Conservative Party leader Jackson Carlaw quit after only six months in

July 2020 when polls revealed that he was failing to halt the growing popularity of the Scottish National Party.[41] In another example, the UK Labour Party leader at the time of writing, Sir Keir Starmer, gives press statements in front of a Union Jack because polls showed that a section of Labour's voter base disliked the previous leader Jeremy Corbyn for his supposed lack of patriotism.[42] How many businesses would be bold enough to seek this kind of feedback on the impact of their messages and leaders? Is it worth surveying your customers to identify messages which resonate with them and adapt your strategy and PR accordingly?

It is certainly worth considering surveys at the start of the PR campaign or the beginning of the year, so you understand your current position. Then repeat the exercise at six- to twelve-month intervals to gauge your campaign's impact.

Survey at mega maritime trade fairs

A brilliant place to undertake surveys is at the big maritime trade fairs around the world. Organisers at SMM in Hamburg send out groups of young people armed with iPads to capture delegates' views of the event. The trade fairs also present a great opportunity for you to speak to the maritime industry en masse face to face and gain invaluable insight into how people regard you and your niche. But – keep your surveys short and quick to complete!

Outputs – social media

There is a fantastic array of reporting tools for social media, but keep things simple and avoid 'data puking', as the industry calls it. You do not want reams of reports which no one reads; you want clear data that tells you about the outcomes and impact you are having.

Start monthly social media reports detailing follower numbers, impressions and top posts. It is important to do this for LinkedIn and Twitter, both of which supply good reporting data that can be exported into reports. Check follower numbers against targets.

What about hit rates to the website? Are they going up with the PR campaign? What are the referral sites? Is your earned media coverage in key maritime titles, for example, taking readers to rich content on your website?

Use Google analytics so you can identify which social media and news websites drive traffic to your website. Then you can target them. (Note: most visits to websites are still driven by Google search.)

Out-takes/outcomes/impact – social media

It is no use simply reporting followers, impressions, likes and retweets in bald numbers; report the conversation you are having on social media. Which journalists and stakeholders are being engaged? What are they saying? Is this aligning to your objectives and gaining support for your messages? What type of themes are most popular? What posts are dud? How can you adapt your campaigns to gain more traction? Is there a time of day when you gain more interest? (I find early morning is best.) Is the social media campaign creating leads and opportunities in line with your objectives?

Out-takes/outcomes/impact – anecdotal feedback

Perhaps the one area most deficient in PR reporting is the collection of anecdotal feedback. Companies must document this critical feedback with their PR firm or communications team so it can be presented in reviews. The customer relations management system or a Google cloud shared between relevant parties can provide vehicles for logging this information, with sections to note opportunities created and feedback received.

Report from the frontline of the business – meetings, trade shows, networking, gatherings with friends and family, and approaches from politicians. Find a way to capture precious pieces of intelligence from these sources – even if it does sound a bit Stasi-like! I have seen campaigns gain greater client buy-in after local and national politicians have requested access to the business as a result of a higher profile and shown a willingness to support the business's clients by writing to senior ministers and asking questions in Westminster.

An example is a maritime client reporting a major deal it had won with the MOD. As a result of sending the PR to the MOD for a quote, the then minister came to visit the company personally to thank the whole team in a company address and took part in press around the visit. This was terrific engagement of a key stakeholder, which created lots of earned, owned and shared media.

Ensure your senior leadership team and sales team ask leads where they heard about the company and feed this back. Then you can document the publications, awards, trade associations and social media platforms that yield the most leads. This is critical to helping show a financial ROI.

In my experience, PR can open a lot of doors, especially if your PR consultant is willing and able to open their contacts book. PR-driven opportunities can come in many forms, from approaches to join stakeholders on a committee, to requests to give a talk to a relevant business group, to simple invitations for a coffee from an influential stakeholder.

Leave room for flexibility in your communications objectives to let PR work its magic and document the benefits you have experienced in this anecdotal evidence section. Polaris once appeared in the *Manchester Evening News,* which led to the owners of a design agency approaching me over LinkedIn to invite me for a coffee in Manchester. This created a pin-ball effect where I went on to meet several new people, one of whom recommended a book by the entrepreneur Daniel Priestley, which gave me the idea for this book. I later met one of our best suppliers, Dean Ford of the Modern Agency, at one of Daniel's coaching events in London. All from one article in the *MEN*. This benefit of PR could not have been envisaged in the communications plan, but the outcome was an expanding of contacts and knowledge, and the discovery of talented suppliers.

PR moves in mysterious, unpredictable ways. Often, it is about putting yourself out there in the media and finding what trade winds catch your sails to help you meet your objectives. But it is important to record all the achievements, so you know the sources and messages that are driving the outcomes and impacts.

CASE STUDY - INTERNATIONAL SAFETY PRODUCTS

Polaris was appointed by the world's biggest marine inflatable lifejacket maker, Liverpool-based International Safety Products (ISP), to support the sale of the business. The two owners were nearing retirement and the prime objectives of the campaign included raising awareness of the business in the international marine industry to attract high-quality buyers and maximise the sale price.

A problem we needed to tackle was the low profile of the business and the lack of recognition of its strong performance. For two and half years, we promoted the ISP's successes to the regional press and international marine media, including key titles like *Boating Business* and *International Boat Industry* that were read by its target audiences. The regional press coverage also proved impactful at reaching international audiences as in-depth interviews were retained online on highly optimised news websites like the *Liverpool Echo*, a factor that prospective buyers from around the world commented on when they googled ISP as part of their due diligence ahead of meeting the owners.

The media coverage consistently focused on key messages around the growth and profitability of the company, its position as a market leader, its trusted status as a business with a thirty-year heritage and the calibre of its client base, including the UK Ministry of Defence, as well as the Australian, New Zealand, South African and Pakistani navies. Importantly, the publicity emphasised the strength of its exports, which accounted for 70 per cent of its sales built on long-standing client loyalty and an established distributor network.

We further deployed press materials on owned channels, such as social media and the company website, and ran a regular e-newsletter to its stakeholders. Other activity included inviting journalists to its popular equipment demonstration days at Liverpool's Albert Dock and providing PR support at trade fairs like the Marine Equipment Trade Show in Amsterdam and the Defence and Security International in London. This ensured its stands were professionally promoted in the media to stakeholders for the first time with press releases appearing on owned, shared and earned media around the shows. We boosted awareness by organising press calls and journalist visits to its stands.

Geoff Billington, ISP director, said, 'In 2013, ISP decided to use an external source to extensively promote and tell the industry and community about the successful business that was undertaken at our factories on Merseyside. We had a low profile, as we did not have our own brand but produced products for global brands, and felt we were doing a lot better than perceived by our stakeholders and customers. We interviewed several candidates and were immediately bowled over by the enthusiasm which came over at our initial meeting with Polaris. Polaris immediately set about improving our external profile. We constantly appeared in the marine press, our MD was featured on mainstream BBC news, we had coverage on Radio City and German TV. When we came to exit the business in 2015, the shareholders recognised the contribution that Polaris had made in helping International Safety Products attract top-class interest in acquiring our business.'

(Details used with kind permission of Geoff Billington, Director, ISP.)

CASE STUDY – ATLANTIC CONTAINER LINE (ACL) ROYAL NAMING

The objectives of this campaign were to boost local, national and international awareness of the royal naming of the new ACL vessel the *Atlantic Sea* by HRH Princess Anne. This would be the first royal naming of a ship on the River Mersey since 1961. They were also to raise global awareness of ACL's new fleet of five container/roll-on, roll-off (CONRO) ships coming into service operating on its North America to Europe route, showing the ships' capabilities, the type of cargo they would carry and which companies could benefit from using them.

Further, the company wanted to generate media recognition for the spectacular nature of the event and encourage the public to attend the naming ceremony and evening fireworks display, raising awareness of ACL's commitment to Liverpool as the christening coincided with the opening of its new purpose-built European head office in the city for 170 staff – the first purpose-built shipping-line headquarters to be built in Liverpool since 1920. The final objective was to engage stakeholders in the PR around the event, including the Shipping Minister and port operator Peel Ports.

The event was reported in the *Liverpool Echo* with a large page lead a week beforehand so the public had time to plan to attend the christening and fireworks display. Polaris guided ACL in communicating key messages around the company's commitment to the city across media, including a sit-down interview with the *Liverpool Echo* before the event. We ensured a range of media attended the christening, reflecting the different audiences ACL wanted to reach, including international media in BBC World TV, regional press in BBC Radio Merseyside, BBC North West TV, ITV Granada TV and the *Liverpool Echo*. In fact, ITV Granada used the fireworks display as the closing pictures of its evening bulletin.

Furthermore, we ensured strong industry recognition of the event by inviting key reporters from the international maritime trade, offering face-to-face interviews with senior management from ACL and its owners, the famous Grimaldi Shipping Group. Publications attending included *Lloyd's List, International*

Bulk Journal and *Freight Business Journal*. Finally, we ensured key stakeholders in the Shipping Ministry and Peel Ports were quoted in the press release and interviewed by the media.

The event encouraged positive engagement from reporters and stakeholders on social media, and a large number of the public were engaged by attending it on Liverpool Waterfront.

(Details used with kind permission of Renee Sisk, PR Administrator, Corporate, Atlantic Container Line.)

Further evaluation

Benchmark competitors to assess how you are performing. You can quite easily benchmark yourself against competitors by setting up a media monitoring service through cuttings agencies like Gorkana, or starting your own in-house monitoring using Google News alerts and harvesting weekly or monthly reports on competitors' social media activity. Your PR consultant can pull all this together for a two- or three-month period to give you an idea of the volume of PR competitors are putting out, the amount and quality of media coverage they are generating and what themes they are focusing on.

PR is a slow burn, and the process of securing outcomes and impacts is different with every business. You need at least six months of consistent PR to make headway; you will then climb further up the ladder of changing attitudes after twelve months, and again after eighteen months. The key is to maintain awareness and momentum. Without profile, you are quickly forgotten.

Key points

- Evaluation is changing. It is no longer enough to 'send stuff out' and collect cuttings.

- Evaluation is the business end of the campaign where you can track progress in line with communications plan objectives.

- Be realistic about what can be achieved. Use evaluation to inform your communications plan objectives.

- Follow evaluation techniques pioneered by organisations like AMEC.

- A prime benefit of evaluation is to adapt and improve the campaign.

- It is the quality, not quantity, of coverage that counts.

- A single article or particular story may have a disproportionate impact on stakeholder attitudes.

- Avoid data puking. Report the conversation you are having on social media, not simply bald numbers.

- Collect precious anecdotal feedback from meetings, trade shows and networking.

6
Harnessing The Power Of The Media

Harnessing the power of the media is fundamental to a PR campaign. The media provides a port-hole window to the world to raise awareness of your business locally, nationally and internationally. Time and again, I have seen PR create a current to sweep clients along, so whenever they enter a room, their stakeholders know who they are and think positively about them. That is the moment PR turns profile into opportunities.

The maritime sector is fortunate to be served by one of the biggest and best trade presses in the world (see appendix on maritime media). But the truth is too many maritime businesses do not fully engage the trade or mainstream press and are missing a huge opportunity to grow awareness and engage a curious media.

Despite grumblings in the sector about sea blindness – the public ignorance of reliance on maritime to transport 90 per cent of visible global trade – the regional and national media is, in my experience, highly responsive to news from innovative maritime businesses. Representatives from the *Liverpool Echo*, Radio Merseyside, BBC North West TV and Granada TV have often told me that their readers, listeners and viewers 'love maritime', while the BBC, Sky, ITV, the *Financial Times*, *Daily Mail*, *Mail on Sunday* and *Daily Telegraph* have all shown a real interest in high-profile Polaris clients such as the Battle of the Atlantic Memorial campaign. The key is to find the right news angles that will appeal to reporters and present them in a concise, crisp way with imagery, background and statistics.

How to engage the media

There are numerous ways maritime businesses can engage the media, from press releases to calls and interviews. But it is my strong belief that if you are dealing with journalists, your company needs a PR consultant or adviser who really understands the rules of the game – a poacher turned gamekeeper who can be your point of contact with the press.

If you run or manage a high-profile business, never put yourself in the position where you do not have an experienced professional managing calls from the media. It is a recipe for disaster if someone who has no knowledge of the dangers of doing so starts talking to the press. Imagine if an inexperienced manager were to give an inappropriate quote to the media about a sensitive topic. This type of 'company quote' can cause untold embarrassment to a business.

Even an experienced PR consultant can find random fishing calls from the media challenging. I recall one reporter from a national newspaper contacting me, asking for help on a client story. I spent a lot of time pulling information together, and then they completely changed the angle of the story. This, of course, irritated my client, but the reporter could not care less. I later found out this reporter had a reputation for being rude and unfair, which made many PR consultants wary of them.

Make reporters' lives easier

However, this was a notably rare exception. My experience generally is that companies can win the media's respect by showing they have gone to the trouble of employing a media specialist who is there to make reporters' lives easier. A press officer who knows how to write newsworthy press releases and will respond to reporters in a timely fashion using their language, showing they understand the constant deadlines reporters operate within, is worth their weight in gold.

There is real value in recruiting a trained journalist into your team. Many take this route into PR after learning their trade in newsrooms. Companies benefit from their expertise and skillset, as managing the media can be like riding on a tiger's back: exciting, but dangerous.

Some of the maritime media may be more interested in technical articles, but news-driven media as well as national and regional press will always be on the hunt for headlines, good and bad, particularly relating to jobs and contracts. If you run or manage a high-profile business, you are fair game to be criticised, but this does not mean you need to shy away. You may not, in fact, be able to hide from a negative story; it is how you handle your bad news that matters.

If you enter the media arena, it is important to have someone who understands how reporters think around you. For example, be careful of taking reporters into your confidence over a friendly lunch with the wine flowing, unless you know them very well. Only open up to reporters you trust, and if necessary, make it clear what you are telling them is off the record. Although some PR consultants and journalists would say 'off the record' does not exist, and many business owners and CEOs have been caught out by being too open, there is a lot to be said for trusting your instincts when cultivating a relationship with a particular reporter. It can be important to brief them on sensitive matters to help build understanding and rapport.

Much will depend on your personal management style. With experience, you will be able to judge how you want to play the relationship, understanding the risks and rewards. Journalists thrive on gossip and rumour, but they too need strong relationships with key contacts to truly understand what is happening and secure scoops and insightful stories.

The media is a champion

It is equally important to recognise the role of the media as a champion. Too many business owners and senior managers are hostile towards or suspicious of the media, perhaps because they have been burned a few times over a negative or inaccurate story.

I often hear comments such as 'Oh no, we do not deal with journalists or a certain local paper. They just print what they want; do not bother speaking to them.' This ranks up there with the dreaded 'But this is the way we've always done it' excuse.

If you shun a certain publication or, worse, the media in general, you risk encountering the very enemy you may fear. And think of all the positive news you are missing out on. All the opportunities to grow respect and understanding of your successes, ethos and USPs, motivate your team with public recognition and help you recruit more talented team members and suppliers.

Reporters are passionate

Proactively build relationships with your local, national and trade press. Reporters are deeply passionate, motivated and knowledgeable people, and many are not that interested in scurrilous gossip and negative stories. I once heard a well-known BBC journalist say this exact thing – he saw tabloid-style journalism as a ball and chain around the profession's neck.

It is important *not* to lump all reporters into one type. For every tabloid reporter there is a deeply knowledgeable business reporter or technical writer who really understands the inner workings of a ship. It is these journalists you want to get to know.

Leave the paranoia behind. Reputable reporters will be interested to meet you and write about your good news, such as contract wins and job creation, particularly if it is presented well with professional pictures and you take the trouble to invite them into your business for face-to-face meetings, tours and interviews.

But it is also true that it's a reporter's job to write hard negative news from time to time, so do not take this personally. A story about job losses, an accident, a breakdown in union talks or a contract loss – this is strong news. It is of interest to the reporter's readers and industry, however much you may not want it reported. It has, after all, been rather acidly said that journalism is printing what someone else does not want printed: everything else is public relations.

The key with a bad news story is to ensure the reporting is accurate and fully informed. The media will 'just publish what they want' if you do not bother to put your side of the argument across and give them the full facts.

It is striking to see how business owners and senior management's opinions change when they positively engage the press with good news stories, and when they meet journalists and hit it off with them. If you have never proactively issued good news or had a strategy for building a relationship with the media, it is unsurprising that you are only likely to hear from reporters when things go wrong. You will then have no contacts or rapport with the reporters or understanding of how to communicate with them to properly deal with the bad story.

Over time, if you engage the media, you will see there is light and shade; there is good and bad news, but if you manage your press relations well, you will generate a great deal more good news than bad. And when negative news does come along, the media will be more understanding and supportive of your business and the good intentions and ethos of the directors within it.

It is worth emphasising here that most big regional and trade titles hold impressive and serious business awards – more evidence that the media is not in a conspiracy against you, but is in fact keen to recognise and shout about your success at these events.

The press release

When you're planning a press release, it is vital to have it produced by a professionally trained journalist. I cringe at the amateurish quality of some press releases from otherwise credible businesses, often written in house to save money. They generally have no clear news angle, yet this is the public face the business wants to show to the world.

In this arena, you want to be at your most professional. To ensure your press releases do you justice, spend the money and employ a trained writer.

What to look for in a copywriter

When I recruit writers, I look for them to hold an ACE:

- Accuracy
- Conviction
- Education

Accuracy: If copy is sloppy and full of spelling errors and missing words, the writer is either not up to it or lazy. There are many of these types of people around, so beware!

Conviction: Keith Richards of the Rolling Stones once gave advice to young guitarists to try and play with feeling. The same is the case with writing. A good writer will write with passion and conviction. And you really need this in a commercial environment if the writer is going to do you justice. It is their job to bring your story alive and make it inspiring and interesting – and it should be immediately evident if they can do this.

If the copy is dull and muddled, the writer is clearly not enthused, and I have seen this even with trained writers. The best copywriting work from Polaris has come when we have really had to bend our backs and dig deep into a business's achievements and heritage, as well as the ethos of its leaders.

Education: Look for writers who have been to journalist college and secured the NCTJ qualification, ideally up to senior level. This means they have at least a few years' experience in a newsroom, usually on a daily paper, and have learned how to write by churning out tens of thousands of words. Critically, this will have sharpened their news sense.

Working for newspapers, reporters are taught to be able to write about anything in an engaging way. The best stories tell themselves, and you can assess the quality of a writer by how well they interpret the more complex or mundane material.

The first rule of writing is to write to be understood. You can gauge how good a writer is by how quickly they grasp a complicated story, and then explain it in plain English. Reporters are told to write like they are talking to someone in the pub and not lose the reader with industry jargon or by showing off with flowery words. Make sure your writer fits this profile.

News pipeline

When you have your professional writer, press officer or PR consultant in place, meet with them regularly to plan and review a pipeline of news for the forthcoming quarter and year.

What makes news? This again is where you want to have the journalist's skillset in your team. Marketing managers play the role of facilitator, enabling writers to interview your team, ideally in PR clinics, and find stories around the business.

Most business owners and senior managers are sitting on a goldmine of news and do not even realise it. Many times, I have been meeting with a business owner or senior manager and pointed out that a new infrastructure investment or contract is a great story, only for them to respond with 'But it's just what we do'.

What your business does is news, but learning what constitutes news value and sharpening a news sense can take years of working as a reporter, being mentored and tutored like a lion cub learning to hunt. And that news sense drives the order and momentum of a press release, ensuring the most interesting and important facts are presented at pace and in a logical order.

I have seen people without a journalistic background charged with writing press releases and really struggling, expending huge effort in writing horribly garbled copy. News writing is an art form. When executed well, it will maximise your news reach. It is worth investing in getting it right.

Expert viewpoints on what journalists look for

What exactly are journalists looking for? I asked some maritime reporters to share their advice for this book, and they have generously done so.

'It's tough to boil down the essence of news and insight into a short, codified guide since the issues are fluid and agendas are ever-changing. But here are few simple points to guide your approach.

'What's new or different? Who's behind it? Why does it matter? And why on earth should anyone else care? If you can't answer all of those with clarity and conviction, don't expect a journalist or editor to have any interest in doing so for you. Go back, start again, and repeat until you've got a story that resonates. It's tough love, but you'll thank yourself for it.'

— Julian Bray, Editor-in-Chief, *TradeWinds*

'My inbox is bombarded day in, day out with all manner of PR puff. I can usually detect when it is worth tapping the "Delete" button within the first two or three words of the subject line, let alone the opening paragraph.

'What I look for are developments that will shape/change the industry or that I know will raise an eyebrow with our readership. The fact is there are something like 1,800 maritime titles around the world, of which I'd posit 1,790 accept or handle a press release in the same way, making for near identical maritime news portals. I try to delve deeper to bring new angles, and crucially, I look to inject the subtle "Dear Reader" element – "this is important to you because…"

'I am not in any shape or form swayed by advertising. If you send me some marketing guff, I cannot guarantee I will run it as a result of your advertising largesse. I value our readers' time – it is precious – they want news, not fluff.'

— Sam Chambers, Editor, Splash247.com

'The biggest mistake PR consultants make is thinking a "dressed up" sales pitch passes for good, or even acceptable content. If it's not something you yourself would find interesting, why should anybody else?

'*The Naval Architect (TNA)* falls into something of a grey area here compared to much of the maritime media. My approach as editor has always been: "Would this interest me if I was a naval architect?" That means I'm not afraid to get a lot more technical than editors of other publications. But I also try to have a holistic remit and take in more tangential aspects of the maritime industry. Most obviously, that means marine technologies, engines, propulsions, fuels, green technologies, etc.

'One thing I tend to steer fairly clear of is too much commentary on the markets, such as *Lloyd's List* and *TradeWinds* give. I don't expect PR consultants to present something heavily technical, but they should realise our readers aren't idiots. I generally prefer they contact me first for a yay or nay before sending something on spec.'
— Richard Halfhide, Editor, *TNA*

'Here at *Ship and Offshore Repair Journal (SORJ)* we look to PR agencies to supply regular updates from their clients, especially regarding new contracts, new items of equipment and personnel moves. The subjects we cover are all aspects of the ship repair, conversion and maintenance industries. However, many of the ship repair yards rely upon *SORJ* to keep them informed about the latest trends within the overall maritime industry – so they can plan their future development plans.

'The main requirement is that press releases should be newsworthy – round-up information is seldom used. This also applies to press visits – news is the key to what is required by the journalist.'

— Alan Thorpe, Editor, *SORJ*

'I believe good PR comes where there really is a story to be told, a case study and some end-user experience. Yes, it is great to hear about new products and initiatives, but it's important for our readers to know how these are being put into practice and solving the problems the industry is facing.

'For me, having a good relationship with the PR team, whether they are in house or external, is important for getting the most out of a story. An introductory note is always appreciated; mass emails often get ignored.'

— Beth Maundrill, Editor, *Port Technology International*

'Press releases land like confetti at a wedding in editorial inboxes; it is difficult to sieve the golden nuggets from the mud and sludge. So I would say get to the point, make sure the news is at the top and that it is clear. That way, if I'm interested, I can read on and add the detail.

'If I get a rambling press release, it goes straight into the bin. I haven't the time to decipher these. And lastly, don't call me to ask if I'll publish the story. It won't make me do it; if anything, it makes me stressed and wastes my time. If it's pertinent and competes favourably with other news, I'll use it; if not, I won't. Ringing me will not change that.'
— Nick Savvides, Editor, *Container News*

As you can see, reporters are very picky about companies offering the wrong type of news and misjudging their tastes, so it is worth employing a trained writer who understands what the media wants.

News ideas

Hard news

Contract wins and deals, new partnerships, infrastructure investments, VIP visits, new appointments, product launches and services, ship orders, steel cutting, ship naming and ship launch ceremonies all come under the heading of hard news. As do any company figures you wish to share – annual turnover, quarterly sales figures, growth in key or new markets, exports figures. But beware: Companies House is a journalists' playground, so ensure your PR consultant is fully aware of what is written in your annual accounts and has a comment prepared in case your profits or losses are picked up by local business titles or national media.

Soft news

This includes charity fundraising, support for local community causes, company milestones and anniversaries of long-serving team members.

Current affairs

Plan to comment on important events and dates – this is a key dimension of PR. Clearly, you will want to be selective and authoritative rather than chasing headlines, so choose news that is relevant to the messages you want to communicate to key stakeholders.

Ensure you have a calendar that can be updated throughout the year. The national media follows Parliament and politics closely as the prime driver of news, so either plan in advance where you will react to national and international events, or time your own news to avoid clashing with these.

Polaris worked with the *Mail on Sunday* as the exclusive national newspaper partner to the Battle of the Atlantic Memorial campaign launch. The newspaper's reporter advised us that we would have to time the launch and press call in Liverpool for the first week of January, before Parliament returned.

Look at the dates for Parliament rising and returning, as well as elections and big international events like the Olympics. When one major event Polaris worked on threatened to clash with the World Cup final, we had to work quickly to change the dates. Critically, try to plan for major policy announcements relevant to maritime so you are not caught napping.

TIP

A good news device for an introduction or headline is to draw on the superlative – the first, fastest, tallest, biggest, longest, strongest, furthest, most advanced, etc ever made.

The trade wind of change

While you will want to promote your standard day-to-day news, it is vital to move with the trade wind of change sweeping through the maritime sector. Specifically, that means searching for news in your business relevant to the hottest innovation topics, such as decarbonisation and dual fuel/electric ships, autonomous shipping and digitisation. These are the trends that are driving much opportunity in the industry. By communicating your expertise in these areas, you can position your business to catch the trade wind being created.

Many maritime businesses are being caught flat-footed by these changes, and it shows in their media and press campaigns, mainly because they are silent on the subjects. One senior maritime executive told me that a seminar had been laid on to explain some of these innovations as a primer for the firm's team, but only a handful turned up. This apathy and lack of curiosity may seem astonishing, but it reflects how old-fashioned some maritime businesses are, perhaps because they fear additional costs, unproven technology and losing the wealth of work that remains with their existing fleet of diesel engine ships.

You cannot afford to close your eyes to the changing world. Even if your directors are nearing retirement, your business is not. If your PR material looks dated and out of step, move fast to change it. Draw on the experience of your talented team and brainstorm how new technologies could impact on and benefit your business. Don't procrastinate – make the time to do this. It will pay back handsomely.

The inertia of some businesses in the sector is certainly not reflected in the maritime media, which positively brims with debate and stories about the breathtaking state of evolution shipping finds itself in. There is a world of opportunity for your business to engage in the debate and find news stories telling how you are adapting to this exciting future.

Maritime thought leadership

Good reference points include the excellent presentations available on YouTube by maritime thought-leadership guru Clarksons' Non-executive President, Martin Stopford. Martin lit up a Society of Maritime Industries conference in London with his remarkable presentation mapping out nearly two centuries of shipbuilding technology. His theories are based around the great changes in ship propulsion: how steam replaced sail, which was then eclipsed by diesel engine ships.

It was fascinating to observe how these changes happened gradually over decades, but Stopford was clear we are in the midst of one of the great changes now as diesel ships are gradually being replaced by low-emission gas and hybrid-powered ships.[43]

Another reference point in this fascinating debate is the world's first fully autonomous electric-powered ship, the *Yara Birkeland*.[44] There is lots of PR around this to learn from and comment on, and there are almost daily reports on similar stories of innovation in new forms of propulsion and alternative fuels.

Elsewhere, many of the leading classification societies feature a wealth of material on their website news sections and annual reports, showing how they are working with exciting new technologies. It is worth taking the time to study their news to sharpen your ideas to see how your business could fit with the themes through insights and interpretations.

CASE STUDY – THE ISLE OF MAN SHIP REGISTRY

Polaris client IOMSR is one of the world's leading flag states, accounting for 48 per cent of tonnage sailing under the Red Ensign Group. Working with DNV, it undertook the first remote survey ever during the initial lockdown in 2020.

At the time of writing, it was working on one of the first bulk carriers to deploy sails as a form of propulsion. It had also recently become the first flag state to join the Getting to Zero Coalition and launch a seafarer welfare app. Promoting these stories, IOMSR thrust itself to the forefront of the industry as one of the most forward-thinking registries, giving confidence to customers and stakeholders that it is equipped for the future.

(Details used with kind permission of Cameron Mitchell, Director, IOMSR.)

CASE STUDY – SRO SOLUTIONS

Another Manchester-based client, SRO Solutions is a specialist in installing and operating IBM's Maximo asset management software, reckoned to be the most advanced and heavily invested in technology of its kind in the world. SRO is helping drive the digitisation agenda by installing upgrades to asset management systems of some of the biggest companies in the maritime and offshore sector, including Stena Drilling, MODEC and the British Antarctic Survey.

A recent press release Polaris issued for SRO showcased a 14-month high-value contract to replace the asset management software system on six vessels operated by Stena Drilling. The press release reported that the job involved consolidating vast amounts of data from the company's onshore headquarters in Aberdeen and its fleet into one single platform. This included 7,500 unique pieces of equipment on each vessel and 1.2 million historical work orders.

The press coverage was able to show the huge cash savings and efficiencies the upgrade has made. The PR struck a chord with the media and generated more than 20 articles in the maritime and regional press, reaching 2 million readers in key titles *Digital Ship* and *Maritime Optimisation* that are read by stakeholders.

(Details used with kind permission of Tony Lackey, Director, SRO Solutions and Bentley Systems.)

How to structure a press release

Once you have your topics, you want to ensure your press releases are well presented and structured. Here is a template and approach we use at Polaris:

The release should begin with:

- News release from <company name>, location, brief description of what company does
- Website address, Twitter handle, LinkedIn address
- Release date: month, date, year
- Media contact: add name of PR consultant, along with their email address and telephone numbers

Then use a short but strong headline, identifying the company name, location and news peg (also known as the story hook). For example: 'Birkenhead patrol boat maker XLM strikes first deal with Pakistan Navy'.

Keep the intro to no more than 30 words. A good intro will capture the story in one punchy sentence. Superlatives are an effective way of describing your news in an engaging way. Give the language bite by keeping it active, in the current tense, rather than passive past tense, for example: 'Leading Gdansk-based ship engine supplier Ocean Turbos is announcing its first deal in China with Shanghai's biggest shipping company' or 'Geneva-based ship-management company Vortex is reporting its strongest ever year of trading'.

TIP

Think of tweaking the headline and intro to appeal to each type of media. Company location may be central to local press, for example, but less relevant to international maritime media.

Separate the release narrative into two halves

At Polaris we favour the first half of the release to describe the detail of the news angle. If it is a contract win, what is being supplied, to whom, where, in what quantity and how did the deal come about? Avoid going into specific figures if they are commercially sensitive. A way around this is to refer to, say, a 'six figure deal'. This way, the reporter has an idea of the scale of the figure.

The structure should follow the pattern of combining the reporting of facts with quotes from the senior spokesperson, introducing this person into the piece early. But be wary of disrupting the flow with too many facts not directly relevant to the deal and your business. Extra in-depth information could be useful to reporters, but reference it in a 'Notes to editors' section at the end of the release.

The second half of the release explains your client or company's USPs. This part of the release reveals why it is a showcase for the business. What gives your business a competitive edge? What do you do that makes you world class and different?

How this section is phrased is particularly important. It needs to be informative, relevant and helpful to readers. Bland sales speak and platitudes will be hacked out by impatient reporters.

TIP

When pitching your press release, be careful to pick the right times. Early morning is usually conference time and mid-morning a time for writing. Daily journalists will be working to certain deadlines during the day, for example 10, 13 and 17 hours, so find out what these are. Weekly papers tend to publish towards the end of the week, so the beginning of the week, when they are looking for new stories, is a good time to pitch releases.

Round up neatly

Round up every release by adding your contact details and web address for readers with a device known as a boiler plate. For example: 'For further information on <Company Name> contact: Tel: XXXX Email: XXXX Twitter: XXXX Website: XXXX'. If there are notes to editors, include these here.

TIP

Add a media centre to your website. This is a handy tool for reporters. Include contact details for reporters to call, and add photographs, graphics, brochures and factsheets which are easy to download. Also include a library of press releases, as well as an option for reporters to register their details to receive future press releases.

Planning press trips

Make sure it is worth the journalists' time

Press trips are exciting ways to demonstrate what your business does and build closer relationships with reporters. Bigger companies like manufacturers that have large sites with lots to see, such as shipyards, can stage them as stand-alone events. For smaller companies, it is worth partnering with a trade body to be part of a trip or give a presentation with other businesses at a hotel or venue.

A standard press trip probably lasts two days, but it usually takes more time with travel, so be aware that it has to be worth the journalists' time, which is under greater pressure than ever with news teams slashed and much more time spent churning out copy in the newsroom. The reporter will want to walk away with lots of material for future news stories and articles.

I advise you to host a standard trip over two nights with up to two days of planned activity. Usually, the media outlet will be prepared to pay for flight, train or other long-distance travel, while looking to you or the event organisers to cover all costs during the trip, including hotel, meals and in-country transport.

On the first night, allow the reporters to gather and leave them to their own devices, ensuring the entire party is accommodated at one hotel. Do not cut corners at any stage; treat reporters with respect and give them the best hotel, transport and food you can afford.

On the first day, pick the reporters up early and make the most of their time. Bring them to your location or a suitable venue and give them a series of morning presentations ahead of lunch, then guide them around your business or collection of businesses. If you are introducing a region or maritime cluster, it is a good idea to find an economist who can kick off proceedings by giving an overview of the country and region and the role maritime plays in it.

Choose presenters who can light up a room

Ensure you get good presenters, not just knowledgeable ones. Too often, presentations are dull or too detailed. Find presenters who can light up a room, not send people to sleep.

Mix the presentations up with expert panels and question-and-answer sessions so reporters are not sitting on their hands, getting bored. Ensure there are plenty of breaks for tea and coffee and networking.

After lunch, you can free the day up to undertake site tours. In the evening, find a top restaurant and join the reporters for dinner. Mix your senior team and press team in with the guests around the table.

On the second day, you may want to focus more on site visits and product demonstrations, allowing reporters the option for a flight home from mid-afternoon onwards.

When journalists travel a long way to listen to and report on presentations that directors have put huge effort into, it is nice for them to feel appreciated – a feeling that is likely to be reflected in their reports. These kinds of press trips are one of the most rewarding parts of a journalist's job, so always go the extra mile.

Expert journalists' advice

I asked Paul Bartlett, the veteran maritime journalist, for his view on press trips. He explained that there are a number of dos and don'ts on both practical and presentation-related issues:

> '**Allow enough time for each presentation and questions.** I've been on some trips where there are eight separate company presentations, sometimes more. By the time you've moved from one location to another, and then back to the hotel to change for an evening

function, you've covered too much ground in one go. Your head is spinning and you've had no time to file any copy. That means a late night or early morning. If the press trip continues the next day, it's a worsening spiral.

'Brief the presenters thoroughly on who's attending from the press. Include their level of expertise, the fact that questions will be probing and journalists from the UK are invariably more inquisitive than French, Dutch, Norwegian or German ones. Also, they won't put up with you side-stepping a question, unless it concerns a commercially sensitive issue.

'Allow some time, if possible, for one-to-one interviews. Some journalists don't like asking questions in front of others because they may be unsure of themselves or they may not wish to give away their angle.

'Virtual meetings and webinars are a poor second to face-to-face meetings and press trips. They're nowhere near as useful from a journalist's point of view and make their job much more difficult for several reasons.

'It is tricky to ask a question because there are usually too many questions to get through in the time allowed. The presenters may offer to answer all questions, but that takes days, and by then, the deadline has been and gone. Obviously, whoever's running the event will choose the easiest/most favourable questions and ditch the tricky ones. Then there is no chance to raise a follow-up point, ask the question again if it hasn't been answered properly, or enter into a dialogue with the presenter afterwards.'

TNA editor Richard Halfhide gave me this advice on press trips:

'The bottom line is whether I can produce an article from it, and preferably multiple articles if it's a longer trip. If the location is somewhere in continental Europe and the itinerary is exciting enough, we can usually justify the expense of the flight, although hotel accommodation/ transport from the airport is appreciated. Further afield is possible – I'd been due to go to Tokyo for Sea Japan prior to Covid-19, but bear in mind editorial budgets are not as hefty as they once were.'

Jake Kavanagh is another well-known maritime journalist who works for the *Marine Professional* and *International Boat Industry*. He gave this advice on press trips:

'I have been going on press trips since 1987 and the fundamental principle remains the same. The journalist isn't just there for the "story of the day"; they are also there to better

understand the company, get to know the
personalities within it, appreciate the selling
points and get hands-on with the product. This
means they will become an unofficial brand
ambassador for the company in the years
ahead.'

Jake says press trips work when something particularly special is laid on which leaves a lasting impression. Where national pride is at stake, this can make
for some fascinating insights into the host country's
heritage.

'For example, a British yacht company
arranged a private viewing of the Crown Jew-
els followed by dinner in the Tower of London.
An engine maker put the press on to a proto-
type motorboat in Sweden as it performed its
first ever public self-docking demonstration.
The automated feat was made even more
memorable as it had to park itself between two
multimillion-pound racing yachts. It all went
well – to the obvious relief of the marketing
team. However, they had placed a professional
skipper near the manual override, just in case.

'Another communications company organised a press trip to the Arianespace centre in
Cannes to see its latest satellite being prepared
for launch, although all press photography
was banned. But these events don't need to
be big or expensive to be remarkable. Another

highly memorable trip was a visit to the UK's Silverstone racetrack, organised by a manufacturing company. After a tour of the workshops, the journalists were divided into teams to assemble and race some model wooden cars.

'Another manufacturer followed a tour of its factory with go-kart racing, and a superyacht builder took journalists on a high-speed RIB ride along the river to its new construction halls nearby. The common factor in all of these events is that everyone bonded with the company as they shared a fun event.

'If you can think of an interactive or social way to highlight what your company does, and if the event is organised with the same professionalism as you run your business, then you will be remembered with great fondness for many years to come.'

Jake's top tips are:

- **Lack of information can lead to confusion,** which doesn't reflect well on the company. The invite pack, usually sent out in advance, should contain the full itinerary, plus the names and official roles of everyone who will be available.

  Photographs and biographies of the people they will meet are hugely useful, allowing journalists to plan who they would like to speak to on a one-to-one basis later. They can also do their homework on what they are going to see and keep the itineraries afterwards to remind them of the correct spelling of places and people's names.

- **Don't overdo it.** The most demanding press trips are 'inward missions'. This is where a trade body or association will invite a team of international reporters to spend a week touring a country and dropping in on various member companies. I have been on several of these, and by day four out of five, the factories and products start to merge.

The usual itinerary is two visits in the morning, and two or even three in the afternoon. The organiser is trying to maximise the journalists' exposure, but often this just overloads them and does not give them enough time to really soak up what each company is about. Pace your press trip as much as you can.

Media interviews

Media interviews are one of the toughest challenges a business owner or company director can face, but if you prepare and perform well, you can present your company positively to a huge audience. You can also protect your business in a time of crisis. Fronting up when something has gone wrong and giving your audience confidence in your company could make an enormous difference to its future, and that of your career.

HARNESSING THE POWER OF THE MEDIA

But media interviews are easy to get wrong. Ronald Reagan had a brush with nuclear war when he tested a microphone by joking about bombing Russia.[45] Microphone gaffes can be manna from heaven for journalists and hilarious for everyone else, providing it does not happen to you. Remember Gordon Brown's bigoted woman gaffe, which was the defining moment of his 2010 General Election campaign?[46]

Find out the interview format

Is it live or pre-recorded? TV or radio? Will you be in the studio with one presenter or in a remote studio? Will you be part of a panel? How long will the interview be? What is the news peg of the interview and what angle will the journalist be taking?

The producer is unlikely to give you the actual questions ahead of the interview, and it can show a lack of confidence when interviewees ask what the questions will be. You must have confidence that you can answer any question, which means...

Fail to prepare, prepare to fail

Never is this truer than in interviews. Even if you are a natural communicator, a media interview can go very wrong.

There was sympathy for the then Green Party leader Natalie Bennett in 2015 when she failed to do her homework and found herself floundering on LBC radio.[47] She conceded she had given an 'excruciating' radio interview as she launched the party's election campaign and attributed her poor performance to a 'mind blank' and 'mental brain fade'. Bennett made the remarks after giving a halting interview on LBC in which she struggled to explain how her party would pay for the 500,000 new council homes it is pledging to build. She told Nick Ferrari the policy would cost £2.7bn, prompting the presenter to ask: 'Five hundred thousand homes – £2.7bn? What are they made of – plywood?' To her credit, she came back much stronger in later televised leader debates, having learned from a chastening experience.

You cannot underestimate how difficult your interview could be. Never leave yourself having to do mental gymnastics under pressure.

Work out three core messages you can weave into any answer

Beef up your material with an anecdote. Having a snappy soundbite and painting verbal pictures can really help nail your point – the power of a story will help grab the listeners' attention. And ensure you have a handful of 'killer statistics' to back up your argument.

Think of the questions you least want to be asked

And have an answer ready for them so you can respond with confidence. Before your first word, take a deep breath. This gives you pace under pressure. Then launch into your answer and set the tone for the interview.

If nerves kick in, speak slowly, breathe deeply and revert to your core messages. Brush up on your vocabulary – articulate speakers always impress – and sound enthusiastic and engaged.

I remember taking a bright politician to an early morning interview and listening to them 'get through it' by 'umming and ahhing' in a dull, monotone voice. It was enough to send listeners back to sleep.

You are in control

Put yourself in the driving seat. You are likely to know more about the subject than the interviewer, so you can steer the interview wherever you want it to go with your prepared messages.

I have seen interviewees just answer the question they have been asked, and then stop speaking abruptly. This makes an interview awkward. Build in your key messages and give longer answers. Help the interviewer fill the time. Have a conversation.

Dazzle 'em with words, not clothes or sweat shine

The workplace has become more informal, but on TV, you want to look your best. Everyone you know will be watching, won't they?

For women, choose a business suit in a solid colour. Men should wear a suit or jacket, and a tie will give you more authority. Avoid finely striped patterns as this can create a flickering effect on television.

Make-up can remove any sweaty shine. Richard Nixon was reckoned to have lost the 1960 US presidential election when he appeared sweaty and shifty compared with the tanned, authoritative John F Kennedy. If the programme producers do not offer make-up, go to the loo and check you look OK in the mirror.

Key points

- Find a 'poacher-turned-gamekeeper' to help you with media relations.

- Understand the different types of reporters.

- Do not take bad news personally.

- The media can be a champion, so take the time to build up relationships with journalists.

- Understand what makes news and what journalists want.

- Embrace innovation and speak the language of the maritime media on decarbonisation and digitisation.

- Carefully plan press trips. Lay on the best you can afford, make it memorable and do not overwhelm reporters.

- Prepare for media interviews thoroughly. Know your facts; arm yourself with key messages, memorable soundbites, anecdotes and statistics. Dress appropriately.

7
Social Media

Social media presents the biggest opportunity for positive public engagement in modern times. That prize is counterbalanced by it posing arguably the greatest threat to companies' reputations.

As social media is now so powerful and critical to PR, it is important that the CEO or owner of a company takes a personal interest in and responsibility for it. Sam Black's respected work *The Essentials of Public Relations* refers to a comment made by the famous businessman and troubleshooter Sir John Harvey-Jones: 'The main activities a company chairman should concern themselves with are strategic planning and public relations'.[48]

If you think how much you see, read about and hear the Prime Minister, you will realise the enduring truth of this statement. Today, it inextricably extends business leaders' responsibilities to social media, but many older executives in maritime admit to being baffled by social media and its terminology. More than one has told me they do not have the 'emotional space' to free up for it. Meanwhile, younger leaders question whether it is worth the effort and express frustration at how distracting it is, lamenting the standard of debate, particularly on Twitter, characterised by an unwillingness to listen to other people's views, as well as the frequently and unacceptably abusive nature of comments.

While I have some sympathy with this viewpoint, executives have no choice but to get up to speed with social media and take an active interest, even if it is only to set and observe the management of their company's account, however sceptical they feel. And while there are many examples of maritime companies and senior leaders that harness social media impressively, notably class societies like DNV, ABS and LR and organisations like Nautilus International and Mersey Maritime, one of the big problems in the communications world is that other companies and their executives are not doing this enough.

LinkedIn, for example, is growing astronomically, and now has 730 million people registered (more than Twitter, which has around 336 million users) with

100 million joining in 2020 alone, and a staggering half logging in daily and encountering content. Nevertheless, according to CIPR trainer and social media thought leader Andrew Bruce Smith, only around eight million of the 730 million user base are sharing content, let alone creating their own. As a result, just a tiny fraction of business leaders are truly harnessing the PR potential of LinkedIn to engage and influence key stakeholders.[49]

At Polaris, our advice to leaders who feel wary of social media is to turn the negative into a positive. Why not lead by example and show how you think communication on social media platforms should look and sound?

The concept of social media is not new – think of it as a rolling news feed made for you. It's your own free broadcasting channel to engage with your stakeholders. The late great Czech leader Vaclav Havel showed the Soviets he loathed how to behave and communicate in public. He inspired millions around the world when he swept to power as the Iron Curtain came down. He charmed people with his good humour and positivity. Havel succeeded by emphasising what Sam Black described as 'the values of public relations – courtesy, good taste, intelligence, decency and above all responsibility'.[50] I think we could all probably agree that more people taking this approach would greatly ameliorate social media.

If you want to take a more considered approach and learn more about how social media works, start by setting up an account and use it for 'listening' before joining the conversation.

Social media plan

Whether you already have social media accounts or are about to start a social media campaign, it is vital to have a plan. This does not need to be *War and Peace*, but you do need to understand why you are taking to social media as a business.

Ask yourself these kinds of questions:

- How will the campaign support the company's overall objectives and communications plan's SMART objectives?

- Who are we targeting?

- How do we ensure the tone of voice and content is consistent with our ethos and values?

- How will we measure the impact?

- How much time and financial resources do we plan to invest and who will undertake the work?

- Which platforms are most suited to our audiences?

Social media policy

Once you have a plan in place, it will be important to write a social media policy for your company.

At Polaris, we encourage business owners and senior managers to approach social media as an opportunity to present their best self. The key is to empower your team with your social media policy, not intimidate or stifle creativity and enthusiasm with a legal straitjacket.

Clearly, social media poses a risk to your business. You need to understand the pitfalls of publishing so you can guide the company and the team. It is advisable when you create the policy, or even if you have one already, to review it with a lawyer and PR professional. As any NCTJ journalism student will tell you, publishing is a legal minefield – copyright, defamation and contempt of court are just some examples of what can wake editors up in a cold sweat. Take time to clearly explain what you can and cannot post legally.

Involve the team

Once you have your outline policy written down, it may be worth holding a mass meeting or series of departmental meetings to engage the team and even suppliers. Seek their input and creativity for your social media policy.

It makes sense to start with expressing the reputational and legal side to social media, being firm with people about using their common sense and not saying anything negative or commercially sensitive about the business in the public domain. No responsible staff member would do this, but you never know when someone might out of naivety, so it is important to emphasise the nature of social media as a sharing platform. Point out that a statement on a personal account can rapidly enter a public domain where journalists and stakeholders could read the comments.

More generally, encourage people to support each other and, where necessary, report irresponsible conduct. Remember that a big challenge of social media is monitoring and policing the vast volumes of content.

Rather than focus on what the team cannot do, emphasise how they can make a big difference. Explain that you are intending to revamp your social media campaign as part of your PR effort and detail what the benefits of this will be for building reputation and attracting new customers and talent. Restate the company ethos, values and objectives and how you plan to promote these. Perhaps you are looking at explaining the company's history of triumphs and adversity overcome – can the team input into these case studies with their personal experiences?

Then encourage the workforce to help spread your message by getting behind the official company social media feeds with their own personal accounts. It is immensely powerful if the workforce speaks highly of the company.

What about content?

A major shortcoming of social media is quality of content. There is far too much irrelevant and poorly written and presented rubbish. The more people that join social media, the louder that noise becomes. But you can pierce through the din with thoughtful, attractive, newsworthy, helpful quality.

Joseph Pulitzer, the American newspaper pioneer, stated his view of how to communicate, and it remains valid for all the people becoming publishers on social media today:

> '...put it before them briefly so that they will read it, clearly so that they will understand it, forcibly so that they will appreciate it, picturesquely so that they will remember it, and, above all, accurately so that they may be wisely guided by its light.'[51]

It is worth referring to these principles whenever you approach a post.

In journalism, the most important role in the newsroom is that of the editor because they are the quality control. They demand rewrites and spike stories if they lack news value, so start thinking like a ruthless editor if you are to make an impact on social media and build a readership. For this reason, it makes sense to invest in engaging the services of professional journalists and PR consultants to help you communicate effectively.

Create HOT content by focusing on heritage, operations and thought leadership

A method for content creation we at Polaris recommend to clients is to make it HOT: build it around heritage, operations and thought leadership. This can be effective at helping you express your values and plan in advance.

Heritage is a natural place to show pride in your roots, capturing the ethos of your company. Do not be afraid to talk about adversity as well as triumphs. All the best businesses have great stories and maritime is steeped in drama, blood and thunder, so dig deep to find those inspiring stories in your company. Many businesses undersell the heritage part of their story.

Polaris' client, the iconic hovercraft manufacturer Griffon Hoverwork, has a large glass-fronted illustrated timeline in its reception, presenting its highlights over the decades. This kind of rich heritage could easily make a couple of years' worth of social media posts. Why not create a timeline for social media with key dates and anniversaries each year – you could even turn it into a reception display, just like Griffon.

Another business, albeit non-maritime, that presents its history in an impactful and inspiring way is Harley-Davidson. I was lucky to visit the museum in Milwaukee, USA and was amazed to read about the innovation and stories of triumph, disaster and comebacks – and then, in true American style, have it sold to me in a shop brimming with baseball caps, t-shirts and all manner of 'merch'!

One problem with social media is how transient it can be, with the life of a post being short, so it is worth considering capturing your heritage into a permanent brochure or coffee-table read. You can then use the material for social media with plenty of evergreen content while making sure all the in-depth research you do into your heritage will be properly documented for future reference.

An enjoyable heritage campaign my team did was to start a 'Polaris Ship Hall of Fame', enabling us to name ten ships we had worked on. We used lots of pictures to show the range of ships and events we had promoted around the world. The mini campaign helped us at networking events as people mentioned it and we felt better understood and appreciated. It also created original content for our website as we added the

Hall of Fame to our 'about us' page. No keyrings or beer mats yet, though!

Operations as a theme gives you plenty of room for manoeuvre. I especially like it as it can present an authentic insight into the day-to-day running of a business.

As well as promoting your press releases and interviews, you can highlight activity which is not strong enough for the mainstream media, but expresses your values to social media stakeholders. Perhaps staff are posting from a trade fair, or you are undertaking a training day, or a staff member has had a baby or got married. Or perhaps you are rewarding a long-standing employee or sending out a big new order. The important factor is to create a consistent narrative around your values and brand voice.

Think about involving your team in this kind of content – if you give everyone recognition, it can go a long way. The best PR puts caring for people at the heart of a company's ethos. I am yet to find a team member who does not appreciate public recognition, and social media is the perfect place for it.

Thought leadership is probably the most underrated of content-creation tools. I am amazed how many brilliant people at the top of organisations do not even post their views and insights on topical issues in maritime, let alone more in-depth advice articles on engineering matters.

LinkedIn, in particular, provides a brilliant platform to engage regularly with friends and contacts who are really interested in your thoughts. I remember working with one CEO who was good with social media and liked to post regularly, mainly sharing and commenting on relevant industry news. I was struck by how many stakeholders told me they read and enjoyed the CEO's social media activity.

Politics – to post or not to post?

Outside your own operations, you may be tempted to enter the political fray, particularly on Twitter. The PR community is split on whether company leaders should stray into the political arena on social media.

At the time of writing, the end of Donald Trump's United States presidency has seen him removed from Twitter, reflecting the power of the platform. Many PR people have strong views on how he used social media and were happy to criticise him for being outspoken, revealing the colour of their political views.

There is a wider belief as ethos takes a bigger role in PR that companies should make their views known on certain subjects. In maritime, these subjects would be global warming and the pollution of the oceans. I agree that these are important issues to take a stand on, but organisations and leaders need to be careful what they choose to campaign on and why.

I would advise you to be clearly non-political, neither swaying to the left or right. Instead, be issue led. CEOs are not politicians, and while they may have strong views on a subject, they represent a broad church of stakeholders around the world so need to be careful about what they say and do.

During the Donald Trump presidency, for example, I was advised by a business group when visiting America not to mention any support or disapproval I may have had for the president as the country was fairly evenly split. The problem with politics is that it is so divisive, which is why some PR advisers prefer CEOs and business owners not to express their party-political views and stay firmly apolitical and neutral.

Generally, I do not feel comfortable with professionals using their social media feeds to lacerate politicians. It can sound like broadcast journalists presenting their opinion as reporting, the assumption being they are right. But political commentary is a highly subjective area and only you can choose how political you want to be, while understanding the risks.

Which platforms to use

It is not strictly necessary to be active on every social media platform. I find the most impactful social media platforms for maritime business-to-business (B2B) companies are Twitter and LinkedIn. Facebook is brilliant for reach and targeted advertising but tends to be more business-to-consumer (B2C) focused, and TikTok is aimed predominantly at a young audience. You may find your time is better spent focusing on fewer channels which engage your stakeholders best.

Let's now have an in-depth look at my two favourites for maritime B2B.

LinkedIn

Perhaps surprisingly, given the prominence of Twitter in the media and the number of journalists on that platform, LinkedIn has far more users. Bought by Microsoft in 2015, apparently because of its enormous amount of data, its more serious 'Facebook for business' image makes its users highly relevant to maritime businesses, and many of the big players have huge followings. There is a conversation going on here that your business and senior executives need to be part of.

Here are some 'hacks' to refresh your LinkedIn profile (reproduced by kind permission of Stuart Bruce, CIPR trainer):

- First port of call is to get your profile in order. Decide if you'll be using your profile to promote your career or your company or both.

- Research how people use their profiles well.

- Use the headline of your profile to promote yourself with an elevator pitch rather than using your job title.

- Use energy words – such as passion, purpose, drive and transformation – to give your headline bite.

- Use an image on the background of your profile, behind your profile picture, to tell your story. Think of deploying a headline over a striking professional image.

- Make sure your profile picture is professional and smart – bin the holiday snap! LinkedIn is formal, so think suit-and-tie networking, compared to the more informal Twitter, where a smart open shirt and jacket will suffice.

- When approaching someone to connect, ensure you use a covering note that is sincere and short, explaining the benefit to them of connecting. No note could be seen as rude.

- Use the 'about' section to build your credibility. Think what you have achieved for your clients, your track record and what you do.

- Use the 'featured' section to showcase your work, including key thought-leadership pieces and notable highlights, and do not forget film. The more people can see and hear you talk, the easier it will be for them to grasp you, your character and style.

Hashtags for LinkedIn

CIPR training suggests using up to three hashtags per LinkedIn post. The key metric is the hashtag follower/content ratio, so use hashtags that have high numbers of followers, but comparatively few people tagging content with that hashtag.

For example, use #publicrelations versus #PR. The former has 3.7 million followers and less content tagged; the reverse is true for #PR, which has fewer followers 29,894, but more content, so #publicrelations is much more impactful. In maritime, #decarbonisation has just 1,600 followers, #maritime 63,000, #shipping 96,000, #MaritimeIndustry 32,000, while #technology has more than 26 million.[52]

Keep in mind that people can also follow hashtags on LinkedIn, so popular hashtags like

#throwbackthursday or #flashbackfriday can be fun ways for your brand to join a wider social media conversation. Official hashtags at the big maritime trade fairs are good for raising awareness and listening to what is going on, on both LinkedIn and Twitter.

Good websites offering insight into the world of hashtags include www.sendible.com/insights/twitter-hashtags and https://blog.hootsuite.com/how-to-use-hashtags.

Types of post

Focus on the 'post' option on LinkedIn rather than the 'article' option, which has become a dud, to engage with your audience. LinkedIn is the only social media platform that likes you to post pdfs and PowerPoint slides. This is 'content fuel' and gets more views and engagement than normal posts on smartphones because a bigger image keeps eyeballs on your content longer, stops people swiping, and LinkedIn likes it because, unlike a hyperlink, it keeps users on the site, so it is actually good to share an old-fashioned 'fax style' pdf press release rather than a link.

LinkedIn also prefers film to be directly uploaded on to content feeds rather than YouTube links and will promote this kind of content more favourably, allowing films up to ten minutes long. Perfect for snappy presentations and thought leadership.

Paid-for content

CIPR trainer Andrew Bruce Smith warns that the era of organic content – gaining traction for free – is diminishing on social media. It is, therefore, wise to get savvy with paid-for content, or at least try some of the functionality via free trials.

For example, you can sign up for a free two-month trial of the Sales Navigator tool on LinkedIn. This enables you to target your content at professionals by job, industry and geography outside your immediate network. After the trial, you spread the cost over days, from one- to seven- to thirty-day periods, and adjust it accordingly.

This tool enables you to make more informed decisions on the type and kind of people you can market to. From here, you can adapt your content to focus on, say, CEOs or financial directors or HR directors in the maritime industry, drilling down by country. The possibilities are exciting, and I advise mixing your organic content with targeted paid-for campaigns.

The LinkedIn Insight tag

According to Andrew Bruce Smith, the LinkedIn Insight tag is the only way of getting detailed insights into the type of person visiting your website, including their job title, who they work for, location, company size, and so on. He says:

'It is important to stress this information is provided in aggregate, ie it is most definitely not personally identifiable information. You won't be able to identify individuals, but it still gives you an idea of the type of visitor you are attracting.'

The LinkedIn Insight tag is a useful tool to help measure the stakeholder engagement of your campaigns. It is essentially a small piece of JavaScript that you can install on every page of your website – similar to, say, Google Analytics' tracking code.

Andrew says if you use Google Tag Manager, you can install the LinkedIn Insight tag in under a minute. To get the Insight tag, you first need to have created a LinkedIn Campaign Manager account. Although this is intended for use with paid-for campaigns, you do not need to spend any money to get the Insight tag code.

Once you have a Campaign Manager account, go to the 'Account Assets' drop down and click Insight tag. You then enter the website you intend to install the Insight tag on.

'Once you have the Insight tag installed and LinkedIn has verified it, you are in business. LinkedIn will then begin detecting any and all visits from LinkedIn members to your site, and they can be visiting from any channel, not just LinkedIn. Once LinkedIn has detected at least 300 unique users, it will then begin sharing with you details of these visitors – job title, who they work for, location, company size, and so on.'[53]

Twitter

Twitter is an immensely powerful tool for maritime businesses, and the abundance of journalists and media outlets on it makes it the go-to social media platform for news. It provides a great vehicle for you to interact with both stakeholders and national, local and maritime reporters from the likes of *TradeWinds*, Splash247.com and *Lloyd's List*, supporting their stories.

Reporters on Twitter

Research by *PR Daily* in 2019 in America found that 83 per cent of journalists list Twitter as the most valuable social media platform.[54] Facebook made second spot, with 40 per cent saying it is the most valuable, though 44 per cent said they plan to use Facebook less. Instagram and LinkedIn will fill that void, with 36 per cent and 29 per cent of reporters planning to use them more, respectively.

Interestingly, more than half – 61 per cent– said they 'usually' or 'always' consult branded social media profiles when reporting on an organisation, underlining the value of committing resource to your Twitter feed.

Optimising Twitter

Twitter was created in 2006 by Jack Dorsey, Evan Williams, Biz Stone and Noah Glass, and launched in July 2006. Jack Dorsey sent the first ever tweet on 21 March of that year. Twitter now has more than 336 million users, and each day more than half a billion tweets are sent.[55]

Twitter has a 280-character limit per post, raised from 140 characters, but it encourages 'multi-thread posts' for longer messages. Two hashtags per tweet is viewed as optimum.

Just three to five per cent of your followers see each tweet you post on average, according to Twitter.[56] This is no surprise, given that it is unlikely that more than 6 per cent of your followers are active on Twitter at any one time. Be aware also that social media is not generally impactful for driving traffic to your website, so do not bank on web-hits from Twitter as a measurement. Google organic search is almost always the biggest driver of traffic. Generally, as CIPR training advises, people use Twitter passively and go to their feeds rather than checking individual accounts.

Tweets which include images, emojis, GIFs and video receive more impressions. An impression on Twitter is the number of times the tweet has been seen. This includes appearing on your followers' timelines and the times it appears in a search or as a result of someone liking the tweet. It does not include the times someone may see the tweet on a third-party platform; it only counts when they see it on Twitter itself.

Consider using your budget to employ a design agency to help you with images and infographics on Twitter, or download an app such as Pic Collage to do it yourself.

Tools for targeting

There are some great techy sites out there to help you track audiences and trends on Twitter. It would be impossible to detail all the gadgetry and functionality available in this chapter, but some good sites include:

SparkToro.com, a whizz-bang platform which identifies how many 'fake followers' – dud, bot, spam, no longer active – an account has, helping you assess its actual reach and impact. It is surprising that some large maritime organisations can have as much as a third of their followers classed as fake.

Followerwonk is an ingenious tool that helps you find relevant accounts to follow and build your own following. This works by allowing you to search users' biographies by job title, interests, location and key word.

Using 'maritime' as a key word brings up more than 23,000 accounts, ranked by most followers. The leading maritime media Twitter accounts by follower numbers are *Lloyd's List*, *Maritime Executive*, *Maritime Reporter*, *Maritime Journal* and *gCaptain*, while organisations like the IMO and UK Maritime and Coastguard Agency (MCA) also feature highly.

Followerwonk helps you analyse the demographics of followers to your account or any other account, showing when followers are most frequently online and where they are located. It further gives each account a 'social authority' score that measures a user's influential content on Twitter. Followerwonk says this goes beyond a vanity score and is not about having influential followers, but about engagement and how many retweets an account receives.

Other social media tips

How often should you post?

Much depends on the time and resources you have and who you are trying to reach. Three to five posts a week on LinkedIn could well be enough, while on Twitter, with only three to five per cent of followers seeing each post, you can in theory issue the same tweet more than once. Quality generally trumps quantity.

BuzzSumo and trending

Perhaps you want to research a hot topic such as decarbonisation for a thought-leadership article. The BuzzSumo website provides interesting insights into trends and how topics are being reported online. You can see which articles by which journalists gain the most traction and when the issue was gaining most social media hits and in the news by month. This can help you to target journalists and publications that carry impact.

For example, a search of 'seafarers' at the time of writing found online reports by Sam Chambers on Splash247.com, Mike Schuler at gCaptain and Bob Jaques at Seatrade, as well as Nautilus International having gained a lot of social media traction. It is often said social media is a good listening tool to gauge mood and what certain people are saying and doing. BuzzSumo can give you extra insight into trends.

Other good websites for digging out trend data include AnswerThePublic.com, which 'listens into autocomplete data from search engines like Google then quickly cranks out every useful phrase and question people are asking around your keyword'. Google Trends also provides useful data around the popularity of subjects over a set period of time.

Asking a question on social media

Taking a poll on social media can be a really good way to engage stakeholders, but you need to be careful, especially in the UK where the great British humour may blow you a raspberry. Polaris has undertaken polls for clients like Liverpool Seafarers Centre on choosing a new logo and the IOMSR when it was choosing the name of its 'Crew Matters' seafarer welfare app, and they worked well at engaging stakeholders. However, we also worked on the 'Name Our Polar Ship' campaign run by the National Environmental Research Council (NERC) which resulted in a Twitter storm being whipped up over the Boaty McBoatface name.

The name was suggested by former BBC Radio Jersey presenter James Hand and went viral, crashing the NERC website.[57] One Spanish wag also suggested the name Blas de Lezo, a Spanish Admiral who'd fought the British during the 1740s and had 'Made great contributions to the nation's undersea research'. Although Boaty McBoatface was the runaway winner with 124,109 votes, NERC said that according to its competition rules, it would have the final say on any name and chose the RRS *Sir David Attenborough*.

Although the poll generated massive awareness and took the project and the maritime industry to a whole new audience, and the NERC team handled it with good humour, the viral reaction was a bit like confronting a bouncer from West Indian cricketer Michael Holding in his pomp. The lesson is there is always a risk of the unexpected when you're asking a public question on Twitter.

Target opinion formers

A good way to build your following and engage followers with your content is to target opinion formers like journalists and industry leaders. Tag them and respond to their posts. It is always worth reposting content from the media to help them gain traction.

When issuing content, ensure you are listening. See what people are saying online about the issues you are discussing, and judge the mood so you do not strike a jarring note by being tone deaf. Be wary of provoking the close-down 'Twitter mob' unnecessarily.

Awareness days

These are now the hot tickets to jump on for social media content. National and international awareness days are essential to plan for, particularly around green energy, climate change, mental health and women in engineering. The days provide an important platform to show your values and the authentic voice of your leaders, and are great at engaging stakeholders.

Notable days in the maritime industry include the World Maritime Day, first held in 1978 to mark the twentieth anniversary of the IMO Convention's entry into force. Celebrations are held throughout the world, usually in September, to focus attention on the importance of shipping safety, maritime security and the marine environment.

Each year, 25 June is the Day of the Seafarer, recognising the contribution seafarers make to international trade and the world economy. The Day of the Seafarer was first celebrated in 2011, following its establishment by a resolution adopted by the Conference of Parties to the International Convention on Standards of Training, Certification and Watchkeeping for Seafarers.

World Oceans Day is held every year on 8 June to raise awareness of the importance of our oceans and the vital role they play in sustaining a healthy planet. A global celebration, it looks to bring people and organisations together in a series of events highlighting how we can all help protect and conserve the oceans.

Originally an idea put forward by the Canadian Government at the 1992 Earth Summit in Rio, World Oceans Day has been organised by the Ocean Project group since 2002. In 2008, the day gained official recognition from the UN General Assembly, a boost in raising its profile and goals.

Other important dates include World Mental Health Day on 10 October and International Women's Day on 8 March. It is worth researching the official UN international awareness days to identify the most relevant ones aligned to your company values on www.un.org/en/sections/observances/international-days.

Key points

- Social media is now so powerful, it falls within the responsibility of leaders.

- If you are unsure how to use social media to best advantage, start by listening before posting.

- Choose the social media platforms most relevant to your stakeholders.

- LinkedIn presents a huge opportunity as only around eight million of the 730 million user base is sharing content, let alone creating their own.[58]

- Create a social media plan so you know what success looks like.

- Empower your team and suppliers with your social media policy and involve them in the campaign.

- Social media provides a platform to promote your day-to-day operations. Use it to engage stakeholders with key messages and recognise your team. Praise them loudly.

- Stand out with thoughtful, well-presented posts. Build HOT content around heritage, operations and thought leadership.

- Plan for relevant awareness days.

- Be careful of divisive party politics. Consider being issue led and politically neutral.

- Do not be tone deaf. When issuing content, ensure you are listening. See what people are saying online. Judge their mood.

- Experiment with social media gadgets to track audiences to your website and identify leading influencers, reporters, topic trends and trend sentiment.

- Get savvy with paid-for content and blend it with free organic content whose reach may be diminishing.

8

How To Prepare For And Handle A Crisis

The hazardous nature of seafaring, shipbuilding and port operations is obvious, which means the threat of a crisis is constant for many businesses. And when things go wrong, it can become a huge national and international news story.

Think about the tragic explosion at Beirut Port in August 2020 when a large amount of ammonium nitrate stored at the port exploded, devastating the city. Causing more than 200 deaths and 6,500 injuries, it did US$15 billion of damage while leaving an estimated 300,000 people homeless. This became the biggest story in the world for several days. We have also seen the *Ever Given* container ship grab international attention by blocking the Suez Canal,[59] while ship groundings, piracy and maritime cyberattacks have regularly hit the headlines in recent times.

The risk of being caught in a crisis is now massively heightened by social media. The public armed with smartphones have become reporters, undertaking vast amounts of newsgathering for media outlets, ironically at a time when newsrooms are cutting back on journalists. During major incidents like terrorist attacks or the horrific explosion in Beirut, it is public recordings that the media are broadcasting, printing and publishing online.

For this reason, it is vital to have a social media risk mitigation policy covering your workforce and any contractors on your ship or site. Ensure they are given clear boundaries detailing what they can and cannot say or share online.

As I am sure you can imagine, handling a crisis is a highly specialist area and could take up a whole book in itself. What I will provide in this chapter is merely an overview.

Why you must plan for a crisis

What I have learned from handling crises in the maritime industry over the years is that the true character of a business and its senior team becomes clear in these moments. How you communicate internally and externally can define how you are perceived. Crises are extremely intense high-stake situations with reputations and the value of the business on the line.

A crisis handled well can improve the standing of your business, as long as you can control what will quickly become the accepted narrative of the event. But coming out of a crisis well requires serious planning, rehearsals and support from the top of the organisation.

Think people first

The advice I shared in the ethos section of this book is critical in managing a crisis. Next to having a plan, the single best piece of advice I can give in a crisis is think people first. At Polaris we have seen CEOs show real empathy in times of crisis and that has lived on in our perception of them, and I am sure we are not alone.

It is vital to show you care, particularly for the people most affected, so think about how you will support all your team. PR is about what you do, what you say and what others say about you, but it is the 'what you do' that is the most important thing – actions speak louder than words.

Often where organisations go terribly wrong in a crisis is in allowing their reaction to make them look selfish and uncaring, particularly towards their customers or the public who have been negatively affected by the incident.

Provide mental-health counselling

It is critical to take care of your team's mental health as part of any crisis management. From experience, I have seen the harm a crisis can bring to a team and it can have a serious impact on people throughout the company at all levels.

This is particularly the case if the crisis results in a lot of negativity towards and criticism of the company or organisation, which can make it a deeply demoralising experience for the teams. The strain of handling a highly pressured high-profile situation on a 24/7 basis can leave conscientious people feeling unfairly blamed or burned-out, causing problems in their home lives and/or with their health.

If the incident has seen injuries or fatalities, you must prepare for the impact that tragic situation will have on the victims' families and the team handling the crisis. I remember working with a reporter who covered the Lockerbie disaster when a deadly bomb exploded in mid-air on Pan Am Flight 103 in December 1988, killing all passengers and crew and eleven residents of the Scottish town below. The reporter had been left deeply traumatised for over ten years after being one of the first on the scene of the crash, to which they then had to return for weeks. The experience caused them to leave journalism.

Although this kind of disaster is mercifully rare, you must ensure you make counselling part of your crisis plan.

Preventing a crisis reaching the media

Some of the best examples of crisis management are when the issue is so well handled, it stays out of the media. A business may react with such speed, the CEO taking charge and briefing a journalist personally about a sensitive issue, showing what action is being taken, that a potentially damaging report never appears. More strategically, a good crisis communications plan will identify reputational risks in advance and put measures in place to tackle them before they become a crisis.

What is a crisis?

A crisis is something that causes extensive damage, leads to social and economic disruption, and involves multiple stakeholders. This means something has to happen to your business that impacts on your sales and ability to recruit or retain employees and customers. In this sense, it is important to understand that while some incidents may be regarded as a crisis, they are actually no more than a passing negative news story. A crisis is when your reputation is at risk of being damaged.

Eight categories of crisis

More specifically, the Chartered Institute of Public Relations has identified eight categories of crisis, and it is worth detailing them here. Businesses can be hit by a crisis from within the company or through outside factors which then affect their operations. This was brought into sharp focus by the Covid pandemic that hit the world in 2020 and how well, or otherwise, businesses responded to it. But whatever the cause of the crisis, the result is the same – the business is under scrutiny and its reputation is at risk. And often the business is being hit by more than one crisis at the same time.

The CIPR has identified eight categories of crisis:[60]

- Act of God – flood, health pandemic

- Technology – computer system breakdown

- Malevolence – cyberattack, piracy, terrorism

- Confrontation – strike, environmental protest

- Skewed values – where the ethics of the business are increasingly challenged by the public on social or mainstream media

- Misconduct – aggrieved former staff member blows whistle

- Negligence – poor safety controls or cyber security

- Business or economic downturn

The crisis plan

When you understand what form a crisis can take, it is important to start pulling a plan together. There are different stages to handling a crisis, but by far the most important is to have a plan.

A big problem is that many companies do not have a crisis plan, and if they do, they do not test it or devote the time to regular training and subsequent reviews. Do not fall into this trap.

The first challenge for the PR and communications team can be to convince the senior management that a crisis plan and team are necessary. Some bosses like to think they have the experience and skill to handle any situation, but a true crisis can overwhelm and humble anyone, no matter how able.

The job of the communications team and the CEO is to realise the threat posed by a crisis and come together to build a plan that embraces the whole company. It is essential to test your plan regularly, too, so you are never in a position where you are blindsided. If you have trouble convincing your CEO that a crisis plan is required, a good idea can be to organise a crisis training drill with an experienced media trainer who can ask tough, searching questions. This baptism of fire can be the ordeal that shows a leader the brutal 'realities of war' and just how important planning is.

Once you have your senior management on board, it is time to start putting the plan in place.

Set up a crisis working group

Draw people from across the business, notably communications, HR, health and safety, and legal. If you have a continuity or other emergency response plan, align the crisis communications plan to that. Use the working group to identify risks in the business to inform your crisis communications plan.

It can be useful to introduce someone from outside the company into your working group. They can offer valuable insight and think differently to people in house. Having a blend of people is key, including a humanist who looks for the people angle and a doom-monger who can help wargame the worst-case scenarios.

Use the group to undertake stakeholder mapping so you identify all organisations and businesses that should be briefed in the event of a crisis. From the working group, you can also establish your crisis communications team.

A big problem is organisations treating crisis planning as a box-ticking exercise. Make it the working group's job to ensure the crisis communications plan is dynamic and regularly reviewed, updated and tested. The Covid pandemic showed just how important this process is, so include what you have learned from any recent events. Ensure there is an audit trail to show why changes have been made and what you have learned.

Pick 'horses for courses' in your crisis communications team

The make-up of the crisis communications team is critical. A 'horses for courses' approach is best, keeping in mind that a good promoter is not necessarily a good manager of bad news.

Pick the right people for the roles either entirely from in house or blending internal people and external PR consultants who are ideally crisis specialists. Your spokesperson or persons should be the best communicators you have available, not just the most senior, and they should be good at showing a caring human response. They must have received media training but should *not* be the coordinator of the communications response. The spokesperson will have enough on their plate handling and preparing for the media interviews. Give the role of organising the response and carefully adapting your crisis communications plan to a dedicated individual and make sure they are given the space and time to do their job properly, supported by a team.

You will need people to log all the media reports, both social and mainstream. They will answer phones and draft and issue statements, as well as respond to social media comments, so think of appointing a lead for each component of the communications response: overall communications, spokespersons, mainstream press, social media, internal communications, monitoring.

Ultimately, someone must be responsible for signing off statements in quick time. If that is the CEO, they must have the time to respond rapidly. If they are buried in other aspects of the crisis, pass that sign-off authority to someone else.

Speed can be everything in a crisis. In the case of a confrontation, for example, you may be under attack from other organisations and your efficiency of response can be critical to counteracting their propaganda, both in mainstream and social media.

Look at societal trends

Use your crisis working group to undertake horizon scanning, looking at issues that could affect the company such as new legislation and trends in society. In maritime, the industry is caught right in the heart of the climate change and clean oceans debate led by global figures like Greta Thunberg, Sir David Attenborough and the Duke of Cambridge. We have seen huge demonstrations in support of Greta Thunberg from young people and future leaders deeply angry about climate change and the world they will inherit.

While shipping is listening to this societal trend and slowly changing, driven by the IMO targets and Poseidon Principles, the change in attitudes does make some maritime organisations vulnerable. Are you out of step with the drive to stamp out fossil fuels and clean up the oceans? Greenpeace, for example, regularly stages anti-fossil fuel protests, and in 2017, 14 Greenpeace activists protested on a coal freighter on the River Rhine, calling for a coal phase-out in Germany. This type of protest could easily focus on any number of ship owners or ports supporting fossil fuels.

There is also the risk that shipping lines could be 'named and shamed' by investigative journalists for not adapting their fleets fast enough to meet the IMO targets. Good reputational management will identify this risk and look to remedy it before it becomes an issue.

As PR is more about what you do than what you say, if you are going green, you actually have to do it. It is the job of a crisis working group to identify if the company is falling dangerously behind the curve in public opinion, creating reputational risk.

Outside the green debate, look at wider operational risks. Do you have an aging fleet of ships which are an accident waiting to happen? What are the facilities like on board your ships for seafarers, given the huge spotlight on seafarer welfare? Do you have a large site with old buildings and equipment that are a looming safety or fire hazard? Is there a risk you may have to close part of your business because of machine learning and artificial intelligence, resulting in job losses in a few years?

In maritime and engineering, work is often contract driven, which means when large contracts come to an end, redundancies may be required if no new work comes in. It is important to develop responses to these scenarios and, wherever possible, mitigate them – remembering that the most effective crisis management keeps stories out of the news.

Crisis communications plan contents

When you have identified the risks within the business, you can start to pull together the plan. But be aware that the plan is only as good as the testing that supports it. It is important to keep it simple with space to develop your response when a crisis hits; it cannot be too tailored to one type of crisis as all are different.

Introduction statement

Set out who owns the plan in an impact statement ideally from your top person. If the CEO writes this, it sets the tone for the whole organisation and makes it clear everyone needs to take it seriously.

I would suggest you make sure your introduction statement reflects the ethos of your business, closely following your communications plan and detailing your values and how you want to be known. You may want to say you intend to be open and honest, offering full disclosure and transparency in the case of a crisis. You will not mislead; you will tell the truth and only put out verified facts. Remember that a crisis handled well can enhance the reputation of a business and strengthen understanding of its ethos and values, as well as the quality of its management.

The statement should also set out the responsibilities and legislative requirements the organisation has. This is particularly important in maritime where there are a multitude of regulations.[61]

Be clear where the document will be held, both on the cloud and in hard copy, so people can access it at all times, but be sure to keep it secure given its highly sensitive nature. Perhaps give the document a general name rather than 'Crisis Communications Plan' in case it falls into the wrong hands. When you are writing it, be aware that it could be leaked, so be careful what you say.

Communications priorities

In this part of the plan, you set out the different phases of the crisis and how you will respond, from identifying the crisis and beginning to manage the peak, to moving to recovery.

Think about how you will organise the communications team when the crisis begins. Where will they be based, keeping in mind they may have to be off site? What equipment, food and drink will they have? Ensure the team has a grab bag of all the passwords they need for website and social media updates, as well as access to the internet and mobile phones; do not let technology trip you up at this critical moment.

Company graphics, factsheets and frequently asked questions (FAQs) together with photographs of senior staff wearing serious expressions in an appropriate setting are essential. You must set the right tone and show you are accurately judging the mood. In a crisis, all other communications must be shut off, such as lighter planned social media posts.

You will want to work out as quickly as possible who will be leading the response to a crisis – your company or other agencies and stakeholders. When the Covid pandemic first hit in 2020, seafarers were trapped on board ships, unable to disembark for long periods, causing in one instance, reported by the media, a suicide attempt. Fortunately, the shipping line in question had been vocal for months about the crew's plight and had shown caring, responsible leadership.

In this type of crisis, a number of organisations can be involved, from the ship owner and management company to the flag state, seafarer charities and the port authority, and they all have a voice. It is important in this situation that all stakeholders are singing from the same hymn sheet. Make it clear who is leading the response and that no stakeholder issues any information to the mainstream or social media without clearing it with that lead party first. Your communications plan can be shared with stakeholders ahead of any crisis so they are aware of the plan and can adapt and feed into it as necessary.

You will also need to clarify who will lead the communications with those stakeholders of your company who are not likely to be directly involved in the crisis but have been identified as important in the stakeholder mapping process. These include customers, investors, suppliers and politicians. Ensure your messaging is consistent as they may talk to each other.

In the initial response, your grab bag should have as a bare minimum short holding statements for the media that will give you breathing space until you can respond to the crisis with more detailed information. This holding statement can simply acknowledge the crisis, saying that you are dealing with it and more information will be available soon. It sends out the message that you are alert and taking the matter seriously.

Think of adding important information to these statements, such as helpline or contact details in case people are worried about the welfare of loved ones. As a rule, have statements and messaging prepared for specific crises that your working group has identified as being relevant to your type of maritime business, including cyberattacks, piracy, groundings, sinkings, accidents and fatalities, site shut-downs, explosions, strikes and former employees with an axe to grind leaking sensitive information to the media. Your communications team can then adapt the crisis communications plan to the specific nature of the crisis, while monitoring the mainstream and social media and reporting back how the crisis is evolving, documenting what you have said and, critically, what other businesses and agencies have said, to which media and when.

It will be important to ensure all reporting is balanced and accurate. We have found opening channels of communication with priority media and editors particularly helpful in this situation, so they become aware you expect all reporting to be accurate and that their news team must come to you for a response. If the media runs an article or broadcast that is unbalanced or inaccurate, request an immediate correction in robust terms with the editor-in-chief. Going to the top shows how serious you are about the issue, and given that your reputation is on the line, you cannot leave anything to chance. A reporter or news editor may not see giving you a correction as a priority unless they hear it from the editor-in-chief.

Any feedback presented as a 'complaint' is most unwelcome to newspaper reporters and editors as they may have to formally explain to their editor-in-chief what they have done to address the complaint. I have found that requesting a correction without having to make a complaint is looked upon much more favourably by journalists. It may be that they had to go to press before you responded as they were under pressure of a deadline, so work constructively with reporters and help them to do their job without dropping them in it.

You may not be able to devote time to each individual news outlet, given the overwhelming number of websites and social media accounts now, so prioritising the media is key. Work out which channels reach your stakeholders best. You can look at earned media outlets like news websites, newspapers, radio and TV, and decide which you want to prioritise for briefings and even site visits and face-to-face interviews with the senior leadership team to show them what you are doing to tackle the crisis.

Your owned media like your website and social media channels will also play a vital role. Here, you can report news in a way that is not at risk of being distorted by mainstream press. Equally, you can correct misinformation and answer important queries using your social feeds.

Consistency of communication is invaluable. Having the same people giving information at a set time and supplying a source such as a single website or Twitter feed where people can get up-to-date information helps simplify and structure your response.

As the crisis develops and peaks, give yourself space to be creative. If you are in a confrontational crisis, you may want to give your team or crew a voice by starting a petition or uploading their authentic quotes on your website and social media, or offering them as interviewees to the media. In addition, the more you can engage third parties such as contractors, lobby groups, local politicians or the public to support your position, the more powerful your response will be.

After a period, you should be able to gauge the 'accepted narrative' of the crisis. You can then plan how to move to the recovery position and resume normal operations. A big review is necessary at this point to work out the way forward for the organisation, learning lessons for future crises and adapting your day-to-day communications to the accepted narrative of how the company has come out of this one.

Your objective is to understand how the event has affected your reputation and people's trust and confidence in the company. If lessons need to be learned, plan activity to show you have learned them. Once again, the most important dimension to PR is what you do, ahead of what you say and what others say about you.

Rehearsals, training and testing drills

Once you have your working group, communications team and crisis communications plan in place, it is crunch time: you must test the plan. Like any sports team, you need to practise before your big game.

Imagine the England cricket team turning up to compete for the Ashes having rarely practised and without a game plan. It is unthinkable (even if performances in the 1990s may have suggested otherwise). The same is the case for crisis management. You must look for your weaknesses so you can improve and adapt your crisis communications plan. Do not be afraid to fail or look stupid; draw learning from this so you mitigate the risk of falling flat on your face during the real thing.

In maritime, there are several ways you can approach practising for a crisis. You can undertake a desk-type training day, or you can get out on site or ship and do it in a live environment. The key is for it to be as realistic as possible.

Specialist organisations with trained journalists can mock up real-life scenarios based on the types of crises you have identified while keeping the details completely secret from you to maintain the element of surprise and ambush. Planned, coordinated multi-agency multimedia attacks can happen in the case of a confrontation crisis, and remember you can be hit by more than one crisis at once. Ideally, you want to test your response to this.

These exercises can be laid on within your organisation or together with stakeholders you are likely to work with in a crisis. And there is a lot of benefit in the latter if, for example, you may need to work with the MCA, the Royal National Lifeboat Institution, the police, fire or ambulance services, classification societies and flag states. It will be important for your top people to be involved, including the CEO and department heads so they are put under genuine pressure, creating the febrile atmosphere of a crisis.

The exercise should test your crisis statements and how well and quickly the communications and senior management team respond to media enquiries as the crisis evolves. Mock press conferences and media interviews for radio and TV work as a feedback exercise as you can play them back and learn how to improve them before doing them again. Never leave your business in the position where senior management have to front up to the media in the heat of a crisis without having experience of giving such intense interviews or received media training.

Having a social media component to a training drill is now essential. It is not easy to test this, given the public nature of social accounts, but systems are able to replicate a social media reaction in a crisis.

Social media is now without question a key battle-ground in any crisis, especially a confrontational crisis. You want the training drill to test your ability to judge whether to respond, defend your position and risk fanning the flames, or stay silent and risk being outboxed – and see what results from each option. Often there is no right or wrong way, but you need to see the implications of both scenarios and how to respond.

Keep in mind that in a confrontational crisis, there may be a highly organised assault on your company from a wide range of activists as well as organisations – a social media propaganda blitzkrieg. The social media component has changed the world, and it has changed crisis management fundamentally. The main-stream press can be whipped into a feeding frenzy by social media, which is still a Wild West of shrill, politicised and frequently unacceptably abusive commentary. Publishing standards and defamation laws that underpin traditional journalism are bulldozed, particularly on Twitter, as the sheer volume of commentary becomes impossible to police and the lines between free speech, abuse and truth become blurred.

Your training will need to expose you to the brutal reality of this game of media murderball and test how well your team can cope with the volume and, at times, extreme nature of social media.

Key points

- The hazardous nature of maritime makes the threat of crises constant for many businesses.

- Understand what is and is not a crisis. A crisis endangers your reputation and ability to recruit and retain staff and clients.

- Provide mental-health support and counselling to care for your people caught in a traumatic or demoralising crisis.

- Ensure your crisis plan has the full support of your CEO and board.

- Set up a working group from each main department to scan the horizon for potential crises which could affect the business, including operations, legislation and changes in society.

- Identifying potential crises in advance can prevent them happening – this is the most effective crisis management.

- Establish a crisis communications team, but choose the right people. A good promoter may not be as effective in a crisis.

- Have a crisis communications plan, but do not make it too prescriptive to one type of crisis.

- Review, test and update your crisis plan with training drills to find weaknesses. You must not face a real crisis without practice.

- Prioritise key media that reach your audience.

- Social media has changed crisis management fundamentally and can be used to blitzkrieg organisations caught in a confrontation crisis with negative propaganda. Make sure you have a good idea of how and if you will respond.

Conclusion

Thank you for taking the time to read this book. I hope it has given you ideas and inspiration to adapt or transform your public relations. Maritime has some of the greatest stories to tell in business – and you must tell yours.

I feel certain that the maritime businesses and organisations that are most open-minded and willing to embrace change are those that will flourish, specifically, by understanding the value of PR as fundamental to your operations, listening to your stakeholders and the industry, and using that intelligence to shape your strategic direction. I hope I have been able to show that one big change, across industries, is the growth of purpose-driven PR. It is essential for maritime companies large and small to get up to speed with this through vehicles such as the United Nations SDGs, to find out what they stand for and believe in. Perhaps you now have some fertile ideas for how you can improve society and the maritime industry for the better. We know that decarbonisation, ocean pollution, seafarer welfare, safety and education are just some of the issues that really matter in maritime. A word of caution, though: avoid purpose washing at all costs; you have to be authentic.

Let's have a quick look back at the topics we have covered in *Making Waves*. After an overview of the maritime sector, we looked in detail at what PR means to this sector, and to industry in general. We learned that it is so much more than marketing and sales; it is integral to the success of a business. But for a PR campaign to work, it is vital that it has the support and understanding of the C-suite.

A tour of company brand and USP showed that ethos is the soul of your company, the life source from which PR messaging grows. Find your ethos and you can weave it into a campaign plan to crystallise your objectives, describe how you are going to achieve them and explain how you will evaluate impact and progress. Always be sure to put caring for people at the heart of your ethos.

A carefully considered communications plan is critical to the success of your PR campaigns. This is the time when you need to get an expert PR consultant on board, so in Chapter Four we had a look at the skills and qualifications the right person for the role must have. Evaluation is the business end of the campaign where you can track progress in line with communications plan objectives, so we had a good look at this very topic in Chapter Five.

In Chapter Six, we gained an overview of how to harness the power of the media, learning from experienced journalists and fascinating case studies. This is an essential but potentially daunting aspect of PR, including media interviews, crafting a good press release and planning an engaging trip for journalists, but the advice in *Making Waves* puts you in a great position to make a success of it. This chapter also covered the trade winds of change sweeping the industry, focusing on the exciting innovations in digitisation and decarbonisation. With an enthused media on board, PR in the maritime industry really can make a huge contribution towards saving the planet.

The influence of social media is not something anyone can ignore in the modern world. In fact, the role it plays in PR is so crucial that a business's social media presence must be the responsibility of the leader. Ensure no leaders in your company are left baffled by this type of media and the terminology surrounding it.

Finally, we navigated the world of the maritime crisis, a 'crisis' being an event that endangers your reputation and ability to recruit and retain staff and clients. The hazardous nature of seafaring, shipbuilding and port operations is obvious, which means the threat of a crisis is constant for many businesses in this sector. And when things go wrong, it can become a huge national and international news story, so make sure you prepare yourself, your leaders and your teams, and any other stakeholders potentially affected by a crisis.

Armed with your learnings from *Making Waves*, you are in a strong position to make a success of PR in the maritime sector. As a parting idea, I'd like to share twelve quick fixes that you can make use of at any time to boost your PR.

12 quick PR fixes

- Upload client recommendations to your website, LinkedIn and Google reviews.

- Start a company YouTube channel. Thought-leadership vlogging is impactful, so upload films to LinkedIn, too.

- Pitch for an award in your industry or local area.

- Exhibit at a trade fair. Secure a speaking slot and invite journalists to your stand to discuss news stories.

- Adopt a charity and embed its ethos in your marketing – website, social media and PR.

- Identify who can be the Richard Branson-style frontman or frontwoman of your business.

- Research networking events for your front person to attend and speak at.

- Plan a social media campaign to be led by your front person based around blogs, vlogs or case studies.

- Continually refresh company brochures.

- Make a short, uplifting company film for your website homepage and presentations.

- Build a contemporary new website full of case studies and news.

- Refresh your networking pitch, highlighting case studies.

I have spent a lot of time researching and reading about PR for this book, but there is still so much to learn in this fascinating industry. I would like to close by recommending the insightful training offered by bodies like the CIPR and AMEC.

One of the big challenges PR consultants face is that they are expected to cover a wide array of disciplines, including crisis management, media relations, internal communications, strategy, digital media, stakeholder engagement, investor relations, events, literature production and media interviews. It is impossible to do all that without committing to training and continual learning.

Generally maritime does need to improve the standard of PR; companies can too often drift into the shadows and prefer a low profile. That is not to say that all do, and there are many maritime organisations committed to excellent PR campaigns, but the low-profile approach of some big players only harms the industry. In today's media-savvy world, dominated by social media, companies need proactive PR campaigns, the courage to stand up and be counted in crisis situations, and the desire not to remain faceless. Maritime will continue to complain about sea blindness unless it can raise its profile in mainstream media and find its industry champions. The old-school attitude of putting operations first and seeing PR and marketing as secondary is obsolete. PR is about reputation management, and every business depends on that for survival. In addition, PR can help you reach new people and new business. This is perhaps the most exciting thing of all: that ability, like a ship leaving an island, to discover new continents and new opportunities beyond the circle of people you know, through the power of mass communication. PR matters; embrace it and see the difference.

I would love to hear your thoughts on the issues discussed in *Making Waves*. You can connect with me on Twitter, @BenPinnington1 #makingwaves, and on LinkedIn at www.linkedin.com/in/benpinnington.

Glossary: Types Of Cargo

Practically all products in use in day-to-day life have passed through the world's ports. And every product requires its own method of transport or packaging.

There are five types of cargo:

Container cargo includes a wide range of items, from toys to televisions and computers, clothing to meat. By loading the goods efficiently, containers can transport large quantities of them simultaneously.

One 20-foot container can hold the equivalent of 300 shopping trolleys' worth of goods.[62] The container's metal walls protect the goods from the elements, while its fixed size means it will fit on a variety of different vehicles, including lorries, train wagons and barges.

Liquid bulk. All liquid products which are transported by big tankers or through a pipeline come under this definition. They include crude, fuel and vegetable oil. Crude oil is the raw material refineries need to produce new goods, such as fuel oil, petrol and kerosene, products that also travel as liquid bulk.

Dry bulk. This refers to cargo that is not packaged separately but is transported in large quantities. Examples include grain, coal, iron ore, cement, sugar, salt and sand.

Often, dry bulk is processed once it arrives in port. For example, blast furnaces use iron ore and coal to produce steel, while yeast is used to make beer or whisky.

Break bulk is cargo or goods that cannot fit in standard-sized shipping containers or cargo bins. Instead, cargo is transported in bags, boxes, crates, drums, barrels or other handling equipment, or rolled, lifted or pushed onto a ship or barge.

Examples of break-bulk goods include parts of wind turbines, reels and rolls, steel girders, structural steel, heavy or oversized goods, manufacturing equipment, construction equipment and vehicles.

Ro-ro refers to 'roll-on/roll-off', indicating how the cargo is discharged and loaded. Ro-ro can be used to describe passenger ferries where owners drive cars on, or large ocean-going ships used to transport vehicles such as trucks, buses and cranes overseas. Enormous ro-ro vessels transport many of these vehicles in one go – some have enough room for more than 8,500 cars.

Appendix: Maritime Media Background

There are many maritime titles to be aware of. I have highlighted some here to give you a flavour of the media landscape.

Lloyd's List. The world's oldest shipping title, its origins dating back to London in 1734, went online in 2013 with big international reach through its well-read 'Daily Briefing' e-newsletter. *Lloyd's List* takes a hard news approach, and its e-newsletter will not feature standard press releases reported widely elsewhere; it wants heavyweight shipping industry news, rather than engineering news, with focus on containers, tankers, dry bulk and the business of shipping: finance, flag states and classification societies. It takes a keen interest in decarbonisation, alternative fuels and digitisation.

In January 2020, *Lloyd's List* magazine was launched under the editorship of Linton Nightingale. The monthly magazine with a circulation of 3,500 combines former publications *The Intelligence* and *Lloyd's List Containers*. Its 100 most influential people in shipping guide, as well as top ten reports on flag states and class societies, makes revealing reading. It also stages several high-profile awards in line with its owner Informa PLC, which specialises in international events and also owns the *Seatrade* magazine and events business. The magazine hosts an entertaining podcast with editor Richard Meade and his team of well-known industry writers such as Janet Porter and Richard Clayton.

TradeWinds is a relative upstart compared to *Lloyd's List*. Established in 1990 and owned by Norwegian publisher NHST with an editorial team based in London, it takes a hard news approach and is selective towards press releases unless they are newsy and from a high-profile business. It focuses, like *Lloyd's List*, on serious shipping news with a daily e-newsletter and weekly print newspaper, as well as glossy quarterly guides and *Business Focus* magazine. *TradeWinds* has a big presence at trade fairs and its Shipowners Forum at major events like Posidonia in Athens and SMM in Hamburg is exclusive and a seriously hot ticket.

With a talented editorial team led by Julian Bray, *TradeWinds* says it aims to get close to the key movers and shakers on the ground in the USA, UK,

Norway, Greece, Singapore, China, India and 'all points in-between'.

Splash247 is an online-only news website with a daily e-newsletter, mainly focusing on shipping-industry-related news rather than the engineering sector. It is edited by well-known maritime journalist Sam Chambers who has a strong social media presence.

Seatrade is part of the Informa PLC Group, along with sister title *Lloyd's List*. Established in 1970, it has built up a large collection of events including Seatrade Middle East and Sea Asia. Following its merger in 2019 with Informa, it now forms a part of a broader Informa Maritime portfolio that includes the Marintec, Sea Japan and INMEX exhibitions, as well as *Lloyd's List* within a separate division.

Seatrade publishes *Seatrade Cruise Review*, a bi-monthly publication focused on the cruise industry and edited by Mary Bond, who also edits the online edition of *Seatrade Cruise News*. *Seatrade Maritime Review* focuses on commercial sectors of the maritime industry and is edited by Bob Jacques, a well-known figure in the sector. The magazine also has an influential and well-read online presence and daily e-newsletter *Seatrade Maritime News*, edited by Singapore-based Marcus Hand.

Tanker Shipping & Trade, Marine Propulsion & Auxiliary Machinery, Offshore Support Journal, Maritime

Optimisation & Communications, Passenger Ship Technology. This group of titles is published by UK-based Riviera Maritime Media and has a stable of key printed titles more geared towards the engineering, shipbuilding and original equipment manufacturer end of the maritime industry. The group has a high profile at the major trade fairs and a busy global events arm, which diversified into webinars during the Covid pandemic.

At the time of writing, Edwin Lampert is the Executive Editor and Head of Business Relations, while veteran maritime writer John Snyder is the Managing Editor with Martyn Wingrove and Rebecca Moore long-standing editors of *Maritime Optimisation & Communications* and *Passenger Ship Technology*.

The Motorship, Maritime Journal and Boating Business are a group of well-known titles published by UK-based Mercator Media. *The Motorship*, established in 1920, is edited by Nick Edström. It covers the world's merchant fleet and is aimed at marine engineers, ship owners, ship builders, naval architects and equipment suppliers.

The *Maritime Journal* is edited by Jake Frith and covers the European offshore and commercial shipping market. *Boating Business* is edited by Katina Read and is aimed at the leisure marine sector, covering 'everything from canoes to high-spec sailing vessels'. Mercator also produces three supplements throughout the year: *Port Strategy*, *World Fishing* and *Green Port*.

Royal Institute of Naval Architects produces seven in-house titles along with a range of supplements that come out throughout the year. Titles include *The Naval Architect, Ship & Boat International, Shiprepair & Maintenance Technology, Offshore Marine Technology, Warship Technology* and the two annual titles *Significant Ships* and *Significant Small Ships*.

Ship and Offshore Repair Journal. Industry veteran Alan Thorpe produces three publications: *SORJ, Ship Repair* weekly e-newsletter and *Port Engineering Management*.

Maritime Reporter and Engineering News. This respected US title based in New York dates back to 1881 and is now published by John O'Malley, with Greg Trauthwein as publishing director. It is part of a stable of other print and online titles, including *Marine News*, which focuses on North American inland, coastal and offshore workboat markets, *Maritime Logistics Professional, Marine Technology Reporter*, maritimepropulsion.com and marinelink.com. It has a high profile at trade fairs.

Maritime Executive is a popular US magazine. It has a well-read daily e-newsletter with a large circulation, which covers a wide range of maritime news not solely focused on shipping. Founded in 1997 and based in Florida, the print title is published six times a year. The *Maritime Executive*'s publisher is Tony Munoz, with a team including Brett Kiel, Allan Jordan and Paul Benecki. It is active and visible at trade fairs.

Digital Ship magazine and website provides the latest information about maritime satellite communications technology, software systems, navigation technology, computer networks and data management. The magazine is published ten times a year.

Port Technology focuses on the ports and terminals sector. Founded in 1995 and edited by Beth Maundrill, the publication has grown into events, webinars and other multimedia content. Its key subject areas include terminals, digitalisation, automation, shipping, global trade, sustainability and the energy transition.

Safety4Sea has a global readership but a niche in reaching the Greek market. It is committed to promoting safer, smarter and greener shipping, focusing on the crew aspect of the maritime industry. *Safety4Sea* hosts annual conferences and runs the Safety4Sea, Green4Sea and Smart4Sea awards.

Offshore Energy Platform from Netherlands-based publisher Navingo is a busy, well-known online title with a large readership and daily e-newsletter. It focuses on energy transition and sustainable solutions in the maritime and offshore energy industry.

Hellenic Shipping News based in Cyprus is a busy news website and e-newsletter focusing on shipping, shipbuilding, ports, marine insurance, shipping law, freights and commodities, and energy-oil.

Drydock, published by the MPI Group based in Surrey, UK, was established in the early 1980s and focuses on ship repair and the conversion industry. It is aimed at ship owners, managers and operators, ship repair yards, and equipment manufacturers and suppliers. Edited by Mark Langdon, it is published quarterly and supported by a news website.

Ship&Offshore is a German publication that caters for the shipbuilding and offshore markets and is the sister publication of *Schiff & Hafen*. Dr Silke Sadowski heads up the editorial team, which also produces a daily online newsletter. The magazine is published six times a year with special supplements *SmartShip*, *Special GreenTech* and *China Edition* being published throughout the year. *Ship&Offshore* also publishes the *SMM Daily News* over the four days (Tuesday to Friday) of the trade show.

HANSA is another German title. Established in 1864, the monthly magazine has adapted over recent years with a refreshed editorial team headed up by Krischan Förster as editor-in-chief. It has broadened its presence in the market through its daily newsletter and digital edition. *HANSA* also produces the newswire publication for the SMM trade show and other special reports throughout the year.

Navy Lookout. Originally established in 2017 as *Save the Royal Navy*, an online campaign to promote the navy in the UK, it has since rebranded with a simpler focus towards news and analysis. *Navy Lookout* is run by civilians with the help of contributors and supporters, including ex-service personnel and academics. The website is funded by reader donations and a small income from Google ads.

Warships International Fleet Review is the only publication of its type to step out of the standard maritime circulation and be distributed on the high street, allowing for a broader readership. Published by Tandy Media Ltd based in Bexhill, Sussex, UK, and edited by well-known journalist and author Iain Ballantyne, it features in-depth analysis on latest developments in the world navies and defence industry, with a focus on the UK and USA. Tandy Media also publishes *Shipping Today and Tomorrow*, a monthly magazine covering all ship segments across the industry, and *Guide to the Royal Navy* every two years.

Janes Group, based in London, is a long-established publisher of magazines in the defence industry. It has four titles that are weekly or monthly, with print and digital versions. *Janes Navy International* focuses on operations, technology and procurement issues in maritime security. *Janes Intelligence Review* delivers intelligence and analysis on international security issues and country risks. *Janes Defence Weekly* focuses on equipment, military geopolitics, forces, organisations and markets of business in its weekly magazine. *Janes International Defence Review* covers all military segments for emerging technologies through to equipment and systems.

Container News is a UK-based website covering all areas of container freight news. It is edited by well-known maritime journalist Nick Savvides.

International Bulk Journal (IBJ), published by Glenbuck Publishing Ltd based in North Wales, and run by Ray Girvan, a former managing director of Informa IBJ, is aimed at the dry bulk industry covering shipping, commodities, port, logistics and equipment. It also stages a well-regarded annual awards event.

Freight Business Journal (FBJ) is the sister publication of *IBJ*, covering all areas of the freight business. A source of information for decision makers and influencers involved in international freight transport and logistics, it currently has a circulation of 8,247.

Tanker Operator. Published since 2002 by Future Energy Publishing based in London, *Tanker Operator* covers new technologies and activities in the tanker market. It reports on topics impacting the maritime industry, from environmental technologies to cyber-security, in print and digital versions with a weekly e-newsletter. It is edited by Karl Jeffery, a seasoned hand in the maritime press.

Marine Professional is the Institute of Marine Engineering, Science and Technology (IMarEST) membership magazine. Edited by Carly Fields, it focuses on trends emerging within the marine sector and 'aims to enhance understanding of the complex technical intersections between the maritime, offshore and science agendas'.

Nautilus Telegraph is the high-quality in-house monthly magazine and news website of the Nautilus International trade union, which represents 20,000 maritime professionals globally, including seafarers. It is currently edited by Helen Kelly.

GCaptain.com is a US-based maritime news website set up in 2008. It reports large reader figures. The website runs a forum that is popular with seafarers and features high on BuzzSumo for articles gaining the most social media traction.

Notes

1. 'The Covid-19 pandemic: The crew change crisis' (International Chamber of Shipping, no date), www.ics-shipping.org/current-issue/the-covid-19-pandemic-the-crew-change-crisis
2. Figures kindly provided by Stephen Gordon, Managing Director, Clarksons Research
3. UNCTAD, *Review of Maritime Transport 2018* (United Nations, 2018), https://unctad.org/system/files/official-document/rmt2018_en.pdf
4. The proceeds from this book will support a memorial in Liverpool to recognise the 100,000 who died in the longest-running battle of the war. For more information, see www.battleoftheatlantic.org
5. D Lague, B Kang Lim, 'The China challenge: Ruling the waves' (*Reuters Investigates*, April

2019), www.reuters.com/investigates/special-report/china-army-navy

6. K Brown, *China* (Polity, 2020)

7. 'Chapter 4: Population change in the U.S. and the world from 1950 to 2050', in *Attitudes about Aging: A global perspective* (Pew Research Center, 30 January 2014), www.pewresearch.org/global/2014/01/30/chapter-4-population-change-in-the-u-s-and-the-world-from-1950-to-2050

8. 'Shipping and world trade: Driving prosperity' (International Chamber of Shipping, no date), www.ics-shipping.org/shipping-fact/shipping-and-world-trade-driving-prosperity

9. Figure reproduced with the kind permission of UNCTAD

10. 'Global marine trends 2030' (Lloyd's Register, no date), www.lr.org/en-gb/insights/global-marine-trends-2030

11. *Global Offshore Wind Report* (Global Wind Energy Council, 2020), https://gwec.net/global-offshore-wind-report-2020

12. Information kindly provided by Stephen Gordon, Managing Director, Clarksons Research

13. J Ambrose, 'China leads world's biggest increase in wind power capacity' (*The Guardian*, 10 March 2021), www.theguardian.com/business/2021/mar/10/china-leads-world-increase-wind-power-capacity-windfarms

14. 'The leading maritime nations of the world' (DNV, 2018), www.dnvgl.com/publications/

the-leading-maritime-nations-of-the-world-2018-128337

15. 'State of the maritime nations report 2019' (Maritime UK, September 2019), www. maritimeuk.org/media-centre/publications/ state-maritime-nation-report-2019

16. *OECD Yearbook 2012* (OECD Observer, volume 2011, issue 5), https://oecdobserver.org/news/ fullstory.php/aid/3681/An_emerging_middle_ class.html

17. 'The leading maritime nations of the world' (DNV, 2018), www.dnvgl.com/publications/ the-leading-maritime-nations-of-the-world-2018-128337

18. 'Merchant fleet' (UNCTAD, 2020), https://stats. unctad.org/handbook/MaritimeTransport/ MerchantFleet.html. Alphaliner provides a constantly updated list of the 100 largest container/liner operators: https://alphaliner. axsmarine.com/PublicTop100. In April 2021, the top three were Maersk (4,124,272 teu), Mediterranean Shipping Company (3,923,188 teu) and CMA CGM (3,026,135).

19. Ibid

20. Information kindly provided by Stephen Gordon, Managing Director, Clarksons Research

21. 'IMO2020 fuel oil sulphur limit: Cleaner air, healthier planet' (International Maritime Organization, January 2021), www.imo.org/ en/MediaCentre/PressBriefings/pages/02-IMO-2020.aspx

22. M Sofiev et al, 'Cleaner fuels for ships provide public health benefits with climate tradeoffs' (*Nature Communications*, February 2018), www.nature.com/articles/s41467-017-02774-9#ref-link-section-d1456e583

23. 'UN body adopts climate change strategy for shipping' (International Maritime Organization, April 2018), www.imo.org/en/MediaCentre/PressBriefings/Pages/06GHGinitialstrategy.aspx

24. 'Getting to zero coalition' (Global Maritime Forum, 2019), www.globalmaritimeforum.org/getting-to-zero-coalition

25. S Black, *The Essentials of Public Relations* (Kogan Page, 1993)

26. 'About PR' (CIPR, no date), www.cipr.co.uk/CIPR/About_Us/About_PR.aspx

27. A Gregory, *Planning and Managing Public Relations Campaigns: A strategic approach (PR in practice)* (Kogan Page, 2010)

28. S Black, *The Essentials of Public Relations* (Kogan Page, 1993); based on a chapter in JF Awad, *The Power of Public Relations* (Praeger, 1985)

29. Steve Jobs, 'Think different/crazy ones' speech (YouTube, 1997), www.youtube.com/watch?v=keCwRdbwNQY&feature=emb_title

30. S Burns, 'How to create a powerful and tangible brand' (*Forbes*, July 2020), www.forbes.com/sites/stephanieburns/2020/07/24/how-to-create-a-powerful-and-tangible-brand/?sh=5b608f5d4544

31. 'The 17 Goals' (United Nations, no date), https://sdgs.un.org/goals

32. 'Reaching new heights for a safer world' (Lloyd's Register Annual Review 2018/19, 11 December 2019), www.lr.org/en-gb/latest-news/2019-annual-review

33. 'Global goals, ocean opportunities' (United Nations Global Compact, 2019), www.unglobalcompact.org/library/5711

34. 'Nor-Shipping takes principled stance' (Nor-Shipping, no date), www.nor-shipping.com/nor-shipping-takes-principled-stance

35. *Global Opportunity Report* (DNV, 2016), www.dnvgl.com/news/new-report-reveals-business-a-key-activist-in-turning-global-risks-into-opportunities-55482

36. G Dietrich, *Spin Sucks: Communication and reputation management in the digital age* (Que Publishing, 2014)

37. Table reproduced with the kind permission of Stephen Waddington, from https://wadds.co.uk/blog/peso-for-marketing-and-pr

38. 'Measurement matters more now than ever before – an interview with AMEC chairman Richard Bagnall' (Muckle Media, December 2020), https://mucklemedia.co.uk/measurement-matters-more-now-than-ever-before-an-interview-with-amec-chairman-richard-bagnall

39. Table reproduced with the kind permission of Johna Burke, Global Managing Director, AMEC

40. D Priestley, *Key Person of Influence*, 3rd edition (Rethink Press, 2014)

41. C Matchett, 'Analysis: Why are the Scottish Tories failing to make inroads into SNP dominance?' (*The Scotsman*, January 2021), www.scotsman.com/news/politics/analysis-why-are-scottish-tories-failing-make-inroads-snp-dominance-3100565

42. P Maguire, 'Is Keir Starmer stalling?' (*The Times*, February 2021), www.thetimes.co.uk/article/5eb7c90e-66c3-11eb-908c-00b0fcb974f6

43. 'IMO's 2050 decarbonisation goals can be achieved, says Stopford' (*Seatrade Maritime News*, 2021), www.seatrade-maritime.com/regulation/imos-2050-decarbonisation-goals-can-be-achieved-says-stopford

44. 'Yara Birkeland status' (Yara Birkeland Press Kit, November 2020), www.yara.com/news-and-media/press-kits/yara-birkeland-press-kit

45. History.com Editors, 'Reagan jokes about bombing Russia' (A&E Television Networks, 2009), www.history.com/this-day-in-history/reagan-jokes-about-bombing-russia

46. P Curtis, 'How Gillian Duffy nipped out for a loaf – but left Gordon Brown in a right jam' (*The Guardian*, April 2010), www.theguardian.com/politics/2010/apr/29/gordon-brown-gillian-duffy-bigot

47. N Ferrari, 'Incredibly awkward interview with Natalie Bennett' (LBC, February 2015), www.lbc.

co.uk/radio/presenters/nick-ferrari/incredibly-
awkward-interview-with-natalie-bennett

48. S Black, *The Essentials of Public Relations* (Kogan
    Page, 1993)
49. Figures kindly provided by Andrew Bruce
    Smith, CIPR
50. S Black, *The Essentials of Public Relations* (Kogan
    Page, 1993)
51. J Pulitzer, 'Additional resources' (The Pulitzer
    Prizes, no date), www.pulitzer.org/page/
    additional-resources
52. LinkedIn search, April 2021
53. Quotes and details used with kind permission of
    Andrew Bruce Smith, CIPR trainer
54. B Winchel, 'Report: 83% of journalists use
    Twitter – but most still want email pitches'
    (Ragan's *PR Daily*, July 2019), www.prdaily.
    com/report-83-of-journalists-use-twitter-but-
    most-still-want-email-pitches
55. '60 incredible and interesting Twitter stats
    and statistics' (Brandwatch, January 2020),
    www.brandwatch.com/blog/twitter-stats-and-
    statistics
56. Figures kindly provided by Andrew Bruce-
    Smith, CIPR
57. 'Boaty McBoatface instigator "sorry" for
    ship name suggestion' (BBC News, March
    2016), www.bbc.co.uk/news/world-europe-
    jersey-35860760
58. Figures kindly provided by Andrew Bruce
    Smith, CIPR

59. M Safi, 'Suez canal traffic jam builds as work to move megaship continues' (*The Guardian*, 24 March 2021), www.theguardian.com/world/2021/mar/24/suez-canal-traffic-jam-builds-as-work-to-move-megaship-continues

60. Details used with kind permission of CIPR trainer Stuart Bruce

61. The UK Chamber of Shipping publishes a number of books detailing maritime regulations, including *Understanding UK Shipping*. The IMO and the Nautical Institute are further good sources of information reports and publications.

62. 'Container gateway' (Port of Antwerp, no date), www.portofantwerp.com/en/container-gateway

Acknowledgements

I am grateful to many people who have helped me with this project.

I would like to thank Lucy McCarraher and Kathleen Steeden at my publisher, Rethink Press, for seeing the potential of the idea and helping me shape the book, as well as Alison Jack for her thorough editing.

I owe a deep debt to the Chartered Institute of Public Relations for its brilliant learning resources, on which I am now hooked. I would especially like to thank CIPR's Jon Gerlis and trainers Alison Arnot, for her input in the comms plan chapter, Stuart Bruce, for his insights into crisis management, and Andrew Bruce Smith, for his help with the social media chapter.

I thank my mentor Rita Hunt for her forbearance, wisdom and encouragement with this book and much more. By a quirk of fate, Rita stepped into my world the same week my friend and past mentor Len Collinson died. My sadness is that the two did not meet, as they would surely have enjoyed each other's outlooks and mastery of conversation.

Thank you also to Samantha Fisk for help with approvals, editing and researching the maritime media section.

I am further grateful to the journalists Paul Bartlett and Jake Kavanagh for their contributions around press visits in the media chapter. Special thanks also to the journalists who gave their time to provide quotes for the book, which is better for their voices: the legendary Alan Thorpe of *Ship Repair Journal*, Sam Chambers of *Splash 24/7*, Julian Bray of *TradeWinds*, Beth Maundrill of *Port Technology*, Nick Savvides of *Container News* and Richard Halfhide of *Naval Architect*.

Special thanks to Natasha Brown at the International Maritime Organization for her help with the maritime introduction chapter, as well as DNV for approving the use of its Maritime Nations research, Clarksons for allowing the use of its respected data, and Johna Burke at AMEC for giving us the green light to use its research.

Thank you also to all our clients past and present for their support, especially those which have featured in this book: Roxtec, the Isle of Man Ship Registry, China Classification Society, Marine Components International, SRO Solutions, Mersey Maritime, ACL, Griffon Hoverwork, Oman Drydock, Cammell Laird, James Troop, International Safety Products, the Society of Maritime Industries and the Port of Gdansk.

I am proud that 20 per cent of profits from this book will go to Polaris' nominated charities, both causes close to my heart: Liverpool Seafarers Centre and the Battle of the Atlantic Memorial.

Sincere thanks to the Polaris team, Milda Cuplinskaite, Rich Morris, Pamela Brown and Jenny Brookfield, for the consistently excellent and reliable work keeping Polaris on a steady course.

Finally, none of this would have been possible without my wife, Katarzyna, and her constant support, critical eye and encouragement. Without her and our children, Harry and Joanna, there would be no light to illuminate the pages I write. Our adventures, especially in Poland and America, have opened my eyes to pastures of gold. I hope the experiences will live on for our children as they will for me. Who knows, maybe the lure of the sea will capture them one day too.

The Author

Ben Pinnington is the founder of British public relations firm Polaris Media. He works with businesses worldwide, including major shipyards, ports, shipping lines, class societies, ship registries, equipment makers and trade bodies. Ben is a trained newspaper reporter, a member of the Chartered Institute of Public Relations, and sits on committees of the Confederation of British Industry and Society of Maritime Industries. Polaris was voted Professional Services Business of the Year at the 2020 Mersey Maritime Awards.

Contact

🐦 @BenPinnington1

in www.linkedin.com/in/benpinnington

🌐 www.polarismedia.co.uk